Mormonism's Temple of Doom

Magick   Mormonism   Masonry

by William J. Schnoebelen
& James R. Spencer

Mormonism's Temple of Doom

by
William J. Schnoebelen
and
James R. Spencer

Published by
Through the Maze
P.O. Box 9017
Boise, ID 83707

Copyright© 1987
William J. Schnoebelen and James R. Spencer
12th Printing, 2005

Acknowledgments

We would like to thank Sharon Schnoebelen and Margaretta Spencer for their help with the manuscript. We wish to thank Jim Close for his financial and moral support.

William J. Schnoebelen
James R. Spencer

Proofreaders Wanted

In 2005, the text of the book was completely reset for publication. This always introduces typographical errors, no matter how careful we are. If you find typos, please email the page number and the error to:

typos@BeyondMormonism.com

All rights reserved. No part of this publication may be reproduced, stored in a retrieval system, or transmitted in any form or by any means—electronic, mechanical, photocopy, recording, or any other—except for brief quotations in printed reviews, without the prior permission of the publisher.

Note for Fourth Printing:

This book has sparked much controversy since its introduction in July, 1987. Many well-meaning Christians have said it is too "hard;" that the information contained in it is so appalling it would be better to leave it in the dark. I understand those feelings, but I disagree with the wisdom of allowing the temple ceremony to go unchallenged.

As a former temple Mormon, I know—personally—the psychological pain inflicted by participation in the blood oaths. Repeated testimony from Latter-day Saints who, have been rescued out of Mormonism by this book, makes it impossible for us to bow to fear. People I trust, people who know both Mormonism and the wiles of the devil, encourage me not to take this book out of publication.

I am aided in this endeavor by scripture. Paul the Apostle told us we should "have no fellowship with the unfruitful works of darkness, but rather expose them." (Eph. 5.11 — NKJ) That is what he did in Ephesus when he burned the articles of witchcraft in the city square—in public view. (Acts 19.19) Later, he would refer to his struggle against witchcraft in Ephesus, likening it to "struggling against wild beasts." (I Cor. 15:32)

My determination to publish *Mormonism's Temple of Doom* was rewarded one year ago in a dramatic and surprising way: The Mormon Church drastically changed the temple ceremony, excising some of the most offensive parts, including the blood oaths and the mocking of Protestant pastors. I am very glad the Church has made those changes. However, it has not gone far enough. **Only the total renunciation of the ungodly ceremony, in all its aspects, will cause me to cease publishing this book.**

James R. Spencer

Special Supplement to the Fourth Printing

An Amazing Revelation

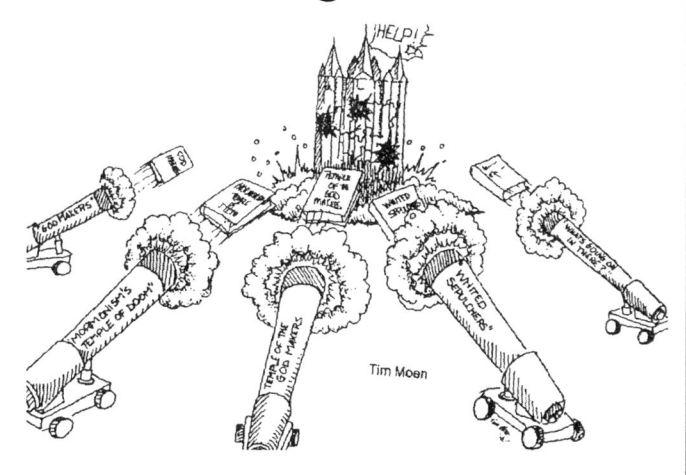

Tim Moen

In April, 1990, the Mormon Church quietly introduced a drastically edited temple ceremony. Many of the changes addressed the very issues raised in *Mormonism's Temple of Doom,* which was originally published in 1987. Gone from the new temple ceremony were the blood oaths, the ridiculing of Protestant pastors, and the infamous "Pay Lay Ale" chant.

Our book no doubt helped induce the changes. This book, along with the work of a host of other Christian ministries forced the Church to either defend or give up the bloody ceremony. I rejoice that Mormonism decided to drop the most offensive parts of the temple

Special Supplement to the Fourth Printing—Page S-1

ceremony. I believe the Church violates its members by pressuring them to participate in the temple ceremony. Thank God, much of the worst of it is now history. I am not naive enough to believe the Church made the changes because it had a change of heart. Rather, I feel the Church was caught red-handed by those of us who had been violated by the temple ceremony ourselves. The Church's position is much like that of a renegade father who quit beating his child after being arrested for child abuse: he slackened the abuse, but his heart is not changed.

It is not that the Church *couldn't* change, but that it *hasn't*. Mormon scripture, for example, still claims that all other churches are *wrong,* that all their creeds are *abominable,* and that all who profess those creeds are *corrupt.* (Pearl of Great Price, Joseph Smith 2.19)

As valuable as this book and other works have been, a more amazing force—a force from within the Church—probably exerted a greater influence for change. Our ministries noted the occult roots of Mormonism and observed the occult practice in the temple, but none of us had any idea how deeply the occult was affecting some individual Mormons. *The fruit of Mormon occultism was to be exposed, not by one of us, but from the highest level of Mormon authority.*

The most amazing Mormon revelation of the last 100 years—perhaps the most amazing Mormon revelation ever

On October 25, 1991 I received a phone call from a man who said an article on the front page of the *Salt Lake Tribune* claimed that Satanic Ritual Abuse was widespread in Utah. I couldn't believe some of the details he was reporting. I was even more shocked when I read the article myself—and the ensuing articles—which were printed in newspapers throughout the country. Investigative television newsmen backed up print journalists.

The *Tribune* said a Mormon General Authority had interviewed more than sixty people who reported witnessing or participating in hideous Satanic rituals. The article reported that Glenn L. Pace, Second Counselor in the Church's Presiding Bishopric, stated that the rituals included "baptism by blood" and that children "were stuffed into plastic bags and immersed in water." The rituals even included "human sacrifice" (reported by *45* of the victims of the abuse). The rituals were performed by "Mormon leaders, temple workers, and members of the famed Mormon Tabernacle Choir." In addition, many of the rituals were "imitations" of some of the temple ceremonies.

The claims were so mind-boggling as to be almost unbelievable. I seriously doubted the charges. But, the Church's public relations spokesman, Don LeFevre, promptly admitted that a twelve-page document on this subject had actually been prepared by Bishop Pace for the "Strengthening the Church Membership Committee." LeFevre also stated that "Bishop Pace was traveling in South America, and unavailable for interviews." As of this writing, he has yet to make a public statement on the matter. However, Utah Governor, Norman Bangerter, authorized a state investigation into allegations of ritual abuse in Utah.

Bishop Pace's document is terribly revealing. His interviews with the alleged victims convinced him that they were telling the truth. (See excerpts from the Pace Document below.) The interviews were conducted over a nearly two-year period. Bishop Pace's

LDS Church
Reviewing
Abuse Claims
Satanic Rituals Copy
Sacred Ceremonies
By Dawn House
The Salt Lake Tribune Oct. 25, 1991

Special Supplement to the Fourth Printing—Page S-3

document is dated July 19th, 1990, demonstrating that the Church had been aware of this problem for at least a year before they announced the changes in the ceremony. It is likely that these revelations—along with the pressure of books like this one—convinced the Church leadership to drop the blood oaths and other especially repugnant parts of the temple ceremony.

Mormonism's Temple of Doom was written to call attention to the occult nature of the Mormon temple ceremony. By exposing these occult practices, we believe we help bring them to an end. When that happens, our Latter-day Saint friends are the clear winners.

—James R. Spencer
January, 1992

Excerpts from the Bishop Pace Document

These quotations are taken from a twelve-page document written by Bishop Glenn L. Pace, Second Counselor in the Presiding Bishopric of the Mormon Church. It was "leaked to the press." Subsequently the Church acknowledged Bishop Pace had, indeed, written such a document.

Ritualistic child abuse is the most hideous of all child abuse. The basic objective is premeditated—to systematically and methodically torture and terrorize children until they are forced to dissociate. The torture is not a consequence of the loss of temper, but the execution of well-planned, well thought-out rituals often performed by close relatives....

The irony is that one of the objectives of the occult is to create multiple personalities within the children in order to keep the "secrets." They live in society without society having any idea that something is wrong since the children and

Special Supplement to the Fourth Printing—Page S-4

teenagers don't even realize there is another life occurring in darkness and in secret. However, when sixty witnesses testify to the same type of torture and murder, it becomes impossible for me, personally, *not* to believe them. ...

Children are put in a situation where they believe they are going to die, such as being buried alive or placed in a plastic bag and immersed in water. Prior to doing so, the abuser tells the child to pray to Jesus to see if He will save her. Imagine a seven-year-old girl, having been told she is going to die, praying to Jesus to save her and nothing happens—then the last moment she is rescued, but the person saving her is a representative of Satan. He uses this experience to convince her that the only person who really cares about her is Satan, she is Satan's child and she might as well become loyal to him....

Just before or shortly after their baptism into the church, children are baptized by blood into the satanic order which is meant to cancel out the baptism into the Church. They will be asked if they understand or have ever felt the Holy Ghost. When they reply that they have, they will be reminded of the horrible things they have participated in and will be told that they have become a son or daughter of perdition and therefore, have no chance of being saved or loved by our Father in heaven or Jesus.

Most victims are suicidal. They have been brainwashed with drugs, hypnosis, and other means to become suicidal as soon as they start to tell the secrets. They have been threatened all of their lives that if they don't do what they are told their brother or sister will die, their parents will die, their house will be burned, or they themselves will be killed. They have every reason to believe it since they have seen people killed. They believe they might as well kill themselves instead of waiting for the occult to do it. Some personalities feel it is the right thing to do....

If you like _Mormonism's Temple of Doom_, be sure to read: _Whited Sepulchers: The Hidden Language of the Mormon Temple_

You won't find any Classic Christian symbols on the walls of Mormon Temples

Whited Sepulchers examines the exterior of the temples, explaining the occult symbolism

Information in the back of this book

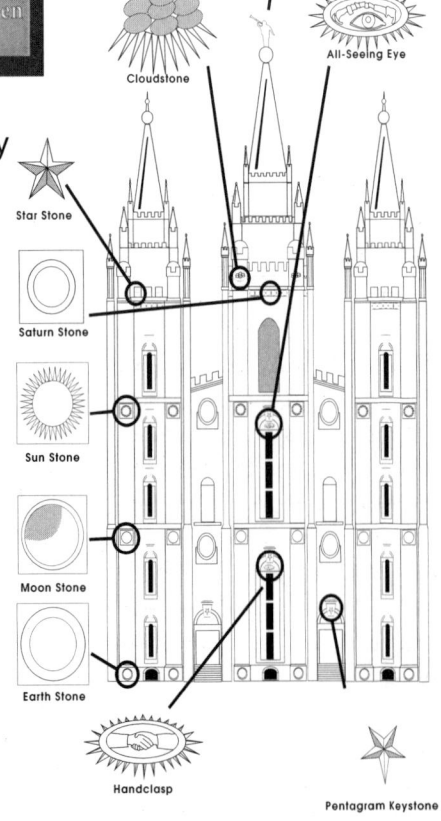

Angel Moroni
Cloudstone
All-Seeing Eye
Star Stone
Saturn Stone
Sun Stone
Moon Stone
Earth Stone
Handclasp
Pentagram Keystone

Special Supplement to the Fourth Printing—Page S-6

Introduction (Spencer)

Many gracious people, who have read my first two books, *Beyond Mormonism: An Elder's Story* and *Have You Witnessed to a Mormon Lately?* (both by Chosen Books), have told me how much they appreciated my compassionate approach to Latter-day Saints. My motive in writing them was to attempt to create an atmosphere in which they could hear the gospel of Christ. In both of those books, I followed the maxim: "Truth without love is too hard; Love without truth is too soft."

My motivation has not changed in this current work. I want to expose the roots of Mormonism which, I have increasingly come to see, are occult. I believe that it is impossible to reach Latter-day Saints effectively until they have lost confidence in Mormonism. That, I believe, requires confrontation. As G.K. Chesterton said:

> "There is a notion abroad that to win a man we must agree with him. Actually, the opposite is true. Each generation has had to be converted by the man who contradicted it most. *The man who is going in a wrong direction will never be set right by the affable religionist who falls into step beside him and goes the same way. Someone must place himself across the path and insist that the straying man turn around and go in the right direction.*"

Bill Schnoebelen originally talked with me about this book at Capstone Conference in July of 1986. I was immediately interested in what he had to say. His unique background brought a clear perspective to what God was already teaching me about false religion: that very little is neutral in the *kosmos*. Whatever ground has not been dedicated by faith to the Kingdom of God, belongs, through Adam's capitulation, to the Kingdom of Hell. That is especially true in religious matters.

Some will doubtless think this is an inappropriate subject for public discussion. That we should leave the banalities and blasphemies of Mormon, Masonic, and Magick ceremony to—as Abraham Lincoln said of slavery—"stink in the dark." But necromancy, like slavery, must be rooted out. If the cults really are the unpaid bills of the church, then exposing Satanic practices (especially when they are done in the name of Christ) is a down-payment on those bills.

This book is written from Bill Schnoebelen's unique perspective as a former witch, Catholic priest, Mason, and Mormon. Bill was as religious as any man could be, as you will see in the documentation at the end of this book. Thank God he was delivered from religion into grace!

I am proud to undertake, with Bill—a man I know to be a warrior of God—in what I think is a project of liberation. Bill and I dedicate this work to those Latter-day Saints who will, because of this effort, "Come out of her"!

James R. Spencer

Introduction (Schnoebelen)

I've been a student of religion and the occult sciences all my life. I was educated in Catholic schools and received a masters degree in Theological Studies from St. Francis Catholic Seminary in Milwaukee. I was, in fact, ordained a priest in the Old Catholic Church—English Rite.

However, like many other "religious" people, I was unsaved. I had not personally experienced the Grace of Christ. I was lost and on my way to hell.

Yet, I continued to study all manner of mystical religions. I became a Master Mason and a Wiccan High Priest. (See documentation at back of book).

Eventually my wife (also a student of the occult) and I investigated Mormonism and joined the Mormon Church. We were True Believers; we "had a testimony" that Joseph Smith was a True Prophet, that the Book of Mormon was scripture and that the Mormon Church was God's True Church.

In due time we went to Salt Lake City to "take out our endowments" in the temple.

My occult background made my first view of the temple ceremony radically different from that of most other Mormons. I was prepared for, and indeed experienced, a spiritual encounter of the highest order—although it was not a godly, but rather an ungodly, encounter.

This booklet documents some of the connections between Mormonism, Magick and Masonry, as they occur in Mormonism's Temple of Doom.

William Schnoebelen

Mormonism's Temple of Doom

The Mormon temple is the spiritual focal point for devout Latter-day Saints. In the temple Mormons are married, their dead are sanctified, and their children are sealed to them for "time and eternity." The most bizarre and distinctive doctrines of the LDS Church are revealed in the temple ceremony. But even though the temple is revered as the holiest Mormon experience, a curious ambivalence about it plagues many Mormons—a mixture of love and dread.

Interestingly enough, a majority of Mormons never go through the temple, and a majority of those who do, never return: less than 25% of all Mormons ever go to the temple at all and, less than half ever return. Only about 6% of the LDS people attend the temple regularly, even though most live within easy driving distance of a temple.

I think these statistics result from the fact that many Mormons are uncomfortable with the temple ceremony. I believe Mormon temple participants are reacting—in their spirits—to the temple rites themselves, which are actually *occult* ceremonies. Those who participate in temple ceremonies unwittingly involve themselves in pagan worship rites, which can cause spiritual—and sometimes *physical*—harm to the participant.

The tragedy is that the people, themselves, are unaware of their occult involvement. They are merely faithfully following their leaders. These people are victims. They are not seeking occult power or Satanic energy. They are totally unprepared for the baroque, Luciferian temple endowment.

Even though some Mormons attend temple preparation classes, they are told *nothing* about the actual temple rites. Upon entering the temple itself, they are plunged into strange surroundings and ceremonies and expected to swear oaths about secrets and rites of which they are totally ignorant.

One of two things happens: either they submit themselves, in blind obedience, to the Church, and therefore, to the temple experience; or they never return, secretly relegating the temple ceremony to a realm of unhappy, frustrating, and best forgotten experience. Those who do make the decision to accept the temple rites and incorporate this new experience into their lives, do so at incalculable cost to their souls.

Do I exaggerate? Are the ceremonies really that sinister? How dangerous are they to one's spiritual health? Can we believe that these rites are actually of Satanic origin?

Encountering the Mormon Temple Ceremony
When I first went to the temple, I fully expected a highly occult ceremony. For me the occult was not evil, it was simply the way God revealed Himself. Many religious paths contained Truth; Mormonism was the highest way and contained the most truth. And I believed my prior mystical training would be confirmed by what I learned in the temple.

In fact, as a student of witchcraft, I had been told that Mormonism, in the temple at least, taught high-level occult science. Years before I ever encountered Mormon missionaries, my witchcraft mentor, the head of all Druidic witches in North America, told me that the highest form of witchcraft was practiced in the Mormon temples.

So when I went to the Salt Lake City temple, I knew I would be involved in highly "religious" activities.

As my wife and I entered the temple, the atmosphere was electric. We felt strange and heavy "vibes".

The "Shield"

After presenting our "temple recommends" (passes), we immediately were shunted into separate dressing areas—I went to a Washing and Anointing area. After removing all my clothing, my naked body was covered in a thin, white, poncho/sheet called a "shield."

Nudity in religious ceremony was not new to me. In fact, the shield was identical to the one I had worn when going through my initiation into the *witchcraft* Melchizedek Priesthood in Zion State Park outside Chicago. The only difference was that the shield I'd worn in witchcraft was black.[1] I'd been taught that the lower degrees of witchcraft wore black, but the highest degrees wore white. In fact, we used the term "The Great White Brotherhood," to refer to high-level Magi.[2] Since I knew that this was to be a very high initiation, I expected the color to be white.

Washing and Anointing

Wearing the shield, I was led into a little cubicle where my body was first washed and then anointed with olive oil by special temple workers to prepare me for later temple experiences. Witches also believe that anointing of the various openings of the body is necessary to keep out evil spirits. Once again, understand that witches do not think of themselves as evil, or pursuing evil. Rather, we were seeking religious truth. We worshipped the 'God and Goddess"—from whom we erroneously thought all religion derived. We did, however, believe evil spirits existed. In witchcraft our challenge was to conjure and control spirits and use their power without being hurt in the process.[2A]

The LDS anointing ceremony is a procedure nearly identical to witchcraft anointing rites.[3] The only difference is that the witch rites are done male to female with more intimate contact. Of course, the LDS rites are also filled with Biblical phrases to make them sound holy.

The Temple Garment

After the anointing, I was dressed in my "temple garment." It was a one piece garment which extended to just below my knees and was similar to a wide-necked T-shirt on top. Masonic markings of "sacred" significance were stitched over the left and right breast, the navel and the knee. This garment, I was told, would protect me from the power of the Destroyer until I had completed my mission here on earth.

I was amazed at how well the occult symbolism had been carried through on the stitched marks: the temple garment was a textbook study in Luciferian symbolism. I was well acquainted with the Masonic symbols because at a certain point in my Wiccan development, my teachers told me to seek Masonic initiation, so I did. I went through Blue Lodge, and then through both York and Scottish rites all the way to the Shrine—which is as high as most Masons go in the United States. Then, and only then, was I considered "worthy" to receive the "continental degrees" from such arcane European Masonic systems as the Ordo Templi Orientis, the Rite of Memphiz and Mitzraim, Martinism and Palladium Masonry. Here I learned the profound links between Lucifer-worship, Wicca and Masonry.

The Masonic compass is stitched over the left breast of the Mormon temple garment. In esoteric Masonry I was taught that the compass represents the sacred Goddess. This is because the compass is used to describe a circle in geometry, and the circle is the consummate symbol of the Goddess in Wicca.[4] Hence all coven ritual is conducted in a circle. As a matter of fact, the "point" of the sacred coven circle actually is the womb of the high priestess who represents the Goddess. The circle then is a symbol of the Queen of Heaven; and the compass is her chief tool.

In Blue Lodge Masonry the candidate is first initiated by piercing his left breast with the point of a compass.[5] And in all occultism, the left-hand is considered sacred to the feminine, goddess-principle.[6]

Over the right breast of the Mormon garment is a square. The right hand side is masculine and sacred to the Horned God (who we in Wicca eventually learned was Lucifer).[7] The square is sacred to Lucifer because of its phallic connotations, and the Fellowcraft candidate in Masonry is challenged on his right breast by the point of the square.[8]

Not only that, the navel mark of the garment resembles a gauge or ruler, which is the Masonic symbol for the "Middle Pillar" of the Qabalistic Tree of Life.[9] (see Tree of Life chart, p. 44). Just as the right and left hand parts of the body in occultism are male and female respectively;

so the Middle Pillar corresponds to the center of the body—the head, solar plexus, navel and genitals.[10]

Mormonism tells us the temple garment has its origins in the covering of skins God gave Adam and Eve in the Garden of Eden. They are supposedly similar to the Levitical Priesthood garments of the Old Testament. In reality, however, one must go to the grimoires or magickal workbooks of black magicians to find the likes of the Mormon temple garment! (In this work, the spelling "magick" is used, a common practice to separate occult magickal practice from stage magic, or illusion).[11]

The placing of magick talismans in underwear is common in witchcraft.[12] But please bear in mind, this is not a recent idea; it appears in classical grimoires in the British Museum which date back to the 16th century.[13]

The Origins of the Temple Ceremony

Mormon temple rites are often nearly identical to Wiccan ceremonies; just as LDS concepts like "eternal marriage," "plural marriage," and "evolution to godhead" are borrowed from witchcraft. Often *exact* wording is duplicated in the ceremonies of Mormonism, Magick and Masonry.

Ample evidence exists to prove that Joseph Smith stole the temple endowment from Masonry or witchcraft, both of which pre-date Mormonism. Serious scholars date the beginnings of speculative Masonry to 1717.[14] Many of the Mormon temple grips and tokens are absolutely *identical* to Wicca and Masonry. (See various charts).

Consider the following evidence connecting Mormonism to Masonry:

1) The Masonic Legend of Enoch (that Enoch was led to find gold and brass plates containing ancient

records in a hillside vault which is taught in the 13th, 14th, and 21st degrees of Scottish Rite Freemasonry) was available to Joseph Smith in his youth.[15]

2) Hyrum Smith (Joseph's brother) received his three Masonic degrees in Mt. Moriah Lodge #112 of Palmyra, NY, about the same time that Joseph was supposedly receiving visions and visits from God and angels.[16]

3) Official LDS church history informs us that Joseph Smith was made a Master Mason on Wednesday, March 16, 1842.[17] Under a subsection entitled "Inauguration of Endowment Ceremonies," Smith informs us that he first taught the Endowment to the LDS apostles on Wednesday, May 4, 1842; *less than two months* after receiving his Master Mason degree.[18]

4) In Scottish rite Freemasonry, men are anointed priests after the Order of Melchizedek. (19th degree—Sovereign Pontiff).

5) The secret handshakes and rituals taught in the Mormon temple are in many cases identical to those of Freemasonry.

6) *The Five Points of Fellows*hip—a body stance initiates assume in the temple when receiving the Name of the Second Token of the Melchizedek Priesthood—is *utterly identical* to the Five Points of Fellowship with which an initiate receives the ultimate secret of 3rd degree, Blue Lodge Masonry.[18A]

These similarities are enough to convict Joseph Smith of plagiarism. To this day, some Masonic scholars consider Mormon temples to be clandestine (illegally constituted) Masonic lodges.[19]

The New Name

After being washed, anointed, and clothed in my temple garment, I received my "new name." This name was never to be revealed to another (mine was Joseph). Mormons suspect that the Mormon Jesus will use the new name to call them up from the grave on the morning of the First Resurrection. Nevertheless, the husband is permitted to know his wife's new name, and I learned my wife's (Joan), so that *I* could call her up from the grave.

When someone is initiated into a mystery cult, it is common practice to give them a new, secret name. Names are felt to have power over the object named: if you know someone's name, you have power over that person. Magick groups and covens give their candidates secret names to represent a new spiritual identity. Secrecy protects your new status and power.[20]

Secret names thus have a profound implication for the LDS wife. She does not know her husband's name but he knows hers; she, therefore, is cast in an inferior role in a very real, occult sense. Having her "new name, he magickally "possesses" her spirit, her essence. This gives the LDS wife no "spiritual space" of her own. She is like a butterfly trapped in the jar of her husband's secret knowledge.

No wonder so many LDS women are nervous wrecks; the challenges of trying to be a "perfect" mother in Zion to too many children, and the oppression of being in occult bondage to her husband is enough to make them crack. (See: "Utah leads the nation in antidepressant use,) *Los Angeles Times,* February 20, 2002) This is the humiliating magickal legacy of the "patriarchal order."

The Temple Endowment

After a Mormon temple initiate gets his new name and packet of robes, he goes through the actual temple endowment. This is a little initiatic drama which purports to cover the Genesis account of the creation: the temptation and fall of Man. In reality, it is a fractured account, laced with extra-biblical doctrines.

We saw it for the first time in Salt Lake City performed live, like a play. In most temples, movies now replace the live acting except for an "officiator" who demonstrates various rituals.

Hypnosis?

The initiate first sits through an incredibly repetitious and tedious account of Mormonism's creation by committee." The Mormon god, Elohim, sends down Jehovah (the pre-existent Jesus) and Michael (the pre-existent Adam)[21] to create the world. Chuck Sackett, a former Mormon temple worker, who performed more than 1,000 temple endowments, thinks this opening drama may be designed to have a quasi-hypnotic effect on the temple patrons, anesthetizing them to the spiritual shocks to follow:

> "[Temple patrons stay in] one room for approximately one-and-a-half-hours, watching the film and officiator as he pantomimes to a tape recording… [the patron sees] the Creation drama, the Garden of Eden drama, the Lone and Dreary world drama, and the Terrestrial World presentation. This might be described as a consciousness-lowering, mood altering experience. The movie shows rather hypnotic

scenes of volcano and lava flows, the ocean, and animal and flower scenes as the dialog drones through a very monotonous, repetitious description of the six creative periods…During this segment many patrons are asleep, and most are drowsy by its completion.[21A]

Adam and Eve come on "stage" portrayed by a man and woman dressed in white clothing. In the Salt Lake Temple, Elohim and Jehovah come down and give them their instruction in a clever little lighted elevator. They are also played by men in white suits.

Then, suddenly, Lucifer walks in. He has on a black suit and tie and a white shirt, and stands out like a black star amid the bland white uniforms (In film versions of the ceremony he wears a crimson robe with a black overgarment). Around his waist was a satin apron covered with Masonic symbols. (Again, the camera does not give you a close-up of his apron and none of the handshakes or penalties are recorded on film).

"Lucifer" proceeds to lead Adam and Eve into temptation, explaining that it is necessary for her to eat of the forbidden fruit to experience the opposites in life: pleasure and pain, good and evil, etc. Here he is teaching essential Gnostic doctrine.[22] Gnostics believed that it was our destiny to be part of both good and evil, and that this was a necessary part of our development. This LDS dogma comes from the Book of Mormon:

> "For it must needs be, that there is *an opposition in all things*. If not so…righteousness could not be brought to pass, neither wickedness, neither holiness nor misery, neither good nor bad.

Wherefore all things must needs be a compound in one." (2Nephi 2:11)

The ancient Gnostic heretics couldn't have put it better. Neo-Manichaeans and the Cathars of medieval times had similar doctrines.[23] In more modern times, the Russian cult, the Khylisti (of which the notorious Rasputin was a member) carried this dualism to its logical conclusion, claiming that one had to sin all possible sins in order to repent properly![24] A central maxim of witchcraft is, "Ye must be willing to suffer in order to learn."[24A]

The final error which Lucifer teaches in this part of the endowment is that "Father" (the Mormon god) had to disobey and eat the fruit in a similar garden in the past in order to attain his godhood. Again, there is not a shred of biblical evidence for this belief; the Bible teaches, in no uncertain terms, that God is sinless and pure. God has not evolved nor is he a man:

"For I am the Lord, I change not; therefore ye sons of Jacob are not consumed." (Mal. 3:6)

"God is not a man that he should lie, neither the son of man that he should repent." (Num. 23:19)

Since the Bible is clear that God is perfect, and since these verses, among literally dozens of others, assert that God is not a man, nor can he change, it is irrational nonsense to think that He ever sinned.

Finally, Lucifer convinces Eve that there is "no other way" for her to evolve spiritually, and she eats of the fruit. He sends her to Adam and instructs her to get him to eat as well.

Adam pompously chastises his wife for eating the fruit and declares his fidelity to "Father's" commandments.

With a doleful countenance, Eve then asks him if he intends to keep *all* of the commandments. He naturally says he will. She then reminds him that...

> "...Father has commanded us to multiply and replenish the earth. I have partaken of the fruit and by so doing shall be cast out, and you will be left a lone man in the Garden of Eden."[25]

Adam, seeing that he is caught in an insoluble dilemma, opts for what seems to be the lesser of the two evils and eats, "...that man might be."

This is, of course, a subtle corruption of the Genesis account. It twists the first sin of our parents into a sort of noble sacrifice. Nowhere does the Bible condone sin. But this strange teaching introduces a dangerous sort of moral pragmatism. LDS authorities have gone so far as to say that Adam "fell upward,"[26] and that "it is not always a sin to transgress a law."[27]

But, be that as it may, Adam eats of the fruit as per the script, and then the unhappy couple recognizes Lucifer for who he is.

The Temple Apron
We then hear Adam ask a somewhat odd, out-of-context question: "What is that apron you have on?"

Lucifer replies, "It is an emblem of my power and priesthoods."

In case anybody missed this assertion, Adam inquires incredulously: *"Priesthoods?"*

Lucifer nods with pontifical finality. "Yes, *priesthoods!*"

Then, without any further discussion of *his* apron, Lucifer commands Adam and Eve to put on *their* aprons. *At this moment the temple initiates are instructed to put on their own aprons. So now we are all decked out in what has just been described as the symbol of Satan's power and priesthoods!* Mormons wear the apron for the rest of the temple ceremony; they are, in fact, buried in full temple clothing, including the Luciferian apron.

The association of the apron with Lucifer and his power goes back centuries in Wicca and occultism. While it is common knowledge that Masons wear aprons, less understood is the fact that most occult and Luciferian lodges wear them as well.[28] Why? Because in magick, the apron is a symbol of magickal energy or planetary (astrological) force. It is the badge of rank for the third degree; and represents (when green) the priestly office of Lucifer. It is the magickal "tool" of that degree.

In this third degree of Wicca, the apron serves a practical, magickal purpose. In this degree, through a bizarre ceremony called the Great Rite, one is initiated into the principles of sex magick (tantra yoga). The apron is often used during this sort of ritual to help contain and channel sexual energy. This is why it covers the genital area. Without going into details, it serves rather like putting a lid on a teakettle to help bring it to a boil. This channelling raises the Kundalini force[29] and supposedly produces enlightenment when the Kundalini serpent strikes upwards and "bites" you metaphysically at the base of your brain.

Additionally, just as the stole is the emblem of authority in the Catholic Priesthood, so the green apron is the emblem of Lucifer's authority. In every Satanic group I knew of, the hierophant (High Priest) always wore a green apron, usually of the finest silk or satin.

Why green? I know that most people's ideas of Satanic rites (which come from garish movies) are that everyone wears black or red (or nothing). This is only partially true. The lower levels wear black, the magi wear scarlet, and the magisters wear white, as was mentioned earlier. But green is Lucifer's color! No one would dare wear it except his "legal" representative: the presiding hierophant.

Green is his color first because it relates qabalistically to Venus. Venus, the "Morning Star," is sacred to him. Alchemically, Lucifer is related to copper.[30] This metal is corrupt within and beautiful without, just like him; and it turns green when it tarnishes.

This concept is more common than most people imagine. It goes very deep in superstitions. For example, people of my heritage (Irish) are very careful never to wear green in any theatrical performance. This is because it is the color of the leprechauns (Satan's little servants) and they fear they will be cursed by them if they wear "his" color.

Rare Satanic documents are available in which the rubrics insist upon the celebrant of Satanic masses wearing a green apron.

All this confirmed what I'd been told years before by my Druidic mentor. In fact, it confirmed the whole metaphysical trap Satan had laid for me. I had joined the Church not only because I believed the Mormon missionaries, but also because I believed it would lead me deeper into occult experience. For a year I had anticipated receiving my temple endowments. Now as I saw Lucifer with his priesthood apron—and as I received my own apron—I was convinced that Christianity reached its highest level of witchcraft in Mormonism. Jesus, I had been taught as a witch, was a Medium of the highest order, who worked miracles by magick. Now as I saw the priesthood of Lucifer transferred to Adam in the apron, I knew it was true.

Temple Oaths
After Lucifer tempts Adam and Eve, the Mormon god Elohim curses Lucifer for his crime, essentially as it appears in the Bible. Lucifer is to crawl on his belly and eat dust. Lucifer snarls back in defiance, "...I will take the treasures of the earth and buy up armies and navies, Popes and Priests and reign with blood and horror on the earth!" He then *walks* out as if God's curse had no effect.

This is very close to the *gnostic* interpretation of the third chapter of Genesis, in which Elohim is depicted as a cunning, impotent spoilsport and Lucifer as the liberating hero, who actually leads Adam and Eve to see the "light." Gnosticism is, of course, one of the oldest heresies to plague Christianity. It has been condemned by many post-apostolic writers, and even by the New Testament writers. [31]

Gnostics saw the God of the Hebrews as a false god (Demiurge) who was enslaving the earth and keeping man from realizing the divine light within him. In most *gnostic* writings, Lucifer moves into Eden as an agent for the true god. He "initiates" Eve into the inner knowledge or gnosis through the Tree of Knowledge of Good and Evil, thereby freeing her from the slavery of the Demiurge (Jehovah)[32]

Likewise, Freemasonry teaches that the Christian God is a demiurge. The arch-Mason, Albert Pike, speaking officially, called the deeds of the God of the Christians "…cruelty, perfidy and hatred of man, barbarism and repulsion for science." He said:

> "Lucifer is God and unfortunately Adonay (the God of the Christians) *also* is God. For the eternal law is that there is no light without shade, no beauty without ugliness, no white without black…pure and philosophical religion is the belief in Lucifer, the equal with Adonay; but Lucifer, God of Light and God of Good, is struggling for humanity against Adonay, the God of Darkness and Evil.[32A]

Secret Oaths and Grips

After this Gnostic instruction, Elohim administers the first of several oaths to Adam and Eve—and to the temple patrons. Eve, because she was "first to eat of the forbidden fruit," covenants to obey her husband's law—"in the Lord." All the women temple participants swear to obey their husbands as gods as long as their husbands obey Elohim. This is called the *Law of Obedience.* Adam (and the men) swear to obey Elohim in the *Law of Sacrifice.* Patrons covenant to sacrifice all they possess, "our lives if necessary," in defense of the Mormon Church.

Initiates then learn the First Token and Sign of the Aaronic Priesthood. (See First Token of Aaronic Priesthood Chart).

The "penalties", or penal signs as they are called in Masonry, all represent grisly methods of having your life taken: throat slit from ear to ear, disemboweling, etc. These penalties are often unnerving in themselves to the naive, young LDS people who take them upon themselves. Patrons are instructed that the oaths are:

> "…most sacred and are *guarded by solemn covenants and obligations of secrecy* to the effect that under no condition, *even on peril of your life,* will you divulge them…"

Temple patrons are told in plain language that when they enact the "penalties' they are depicting *'different ways in which life may be taken."* The Mormon agrees to his own execution if he ever reveals the temple secrets. Documentation of "Blood Atonement" (ritual slayings in Mormonism) is beyond the scope of this document, but ample evidence for such activity is readily available.[33] (See on the Internet: www.HolyMurder.com)

In older versions of the Endowment ceremony, these oaths were more explicit and were implicit permission for murdering Latter-day Saints who had violated or revealed the oaths. In the past half-century the wording of the oaths has been softened.

Such oaths are a violation of Christ's command in Mat. 5:33-37 (see also James *5:12).* Calling upon God to witness blood oaths also violates the Third Commandment:

> "You shall not misuse the name of the Lord your God, for the Lord will not hold anyone guiltless who misuses his name. (Ex. 20.7)

I believe these oaths are extremely blasphemous and incur the gravest spiritual consequences.

The Lone and Dreary World

After taking these oaths, we were led out of the Creation Room and into the 'Lone and Dreary World", or Telestial Room—which represents the world after Adam's Fall. This movement from place to place within the temple is very much in keeping with Masonry and Wicca, for in the Craft, one allegorically spends his First Degree in the ground floor of King Solomon's temple and his Second Degree in its Middle Chamber. (See the Three Temples Chart, p. 42) Similarly, the witch or magician spends his first four degrees on the lower (infernal) triad of the Tree of Life and his next three degrees on the middle triad. (See Tree of Life Chart, p. 44)

Temple workers playing Adam and Eve come on stage and kneel before a Masonic-type altar with scriptures resting on it. Adam raises his hands in a manner identical to the Grand Hailing Sign of Distress of the Master Mason[34] and prays three times: "Oh, God, hear the words of my mouth."

But who should answer Adam's prayer to God? Not Elohim, but *Lucifer!* Here in the Mormon temple, Adam is praying to God, and he is answered by the Devil. *Why should Satan, in Mormonism, have power to answer prayers which are directed to God?*

Adam enters into dialog with Lucifer and there follows a blasphemous little playlet in which a Protestant minister is brought out and mocked as a hireling of Lucifer. The minister eagerly accepts a position in Lucifer's employ—teaching nonsensical parodies of Christian doctrine to gullible Christians. Elohim sends down Peter, James and John (whose appearance is only theoretically possible through Mormonism's unbiblical doctrine of pre-existence) to investigate and ultimately banish Lucifer. They then teach Adam the Law of the Gospel and make some adjustments in the temple clothing. Participants learn the next secret handshake and name. (See Second Token of the Aaronic Priesthood Chart, p. 38).

Before Lucifer leaves (with wounded, tragic dignity) he gets in his last (and best) shot. He turns to the audience of temple patrons and addresses them in a emphatic declaration: "I have a word to say concerning this people. If they do not walk up to *every* covenant they make at these altars this day, *they will be in my power!*"

Even as an enthusiastic new Mormon, those words sent a chill down my spine. Even *my* hardened conscience trembled to hear it. That meant if we didn't keep *every single covenant* that we made in the temple, we were in deep trouble. I didn't understand it at the time, but it meant I was under law, not grace. I've had several LDS people tell me that they were terrified because they weren't certain that they were keeping all their covenants. What a Pharisaical burden to be under. (Mt. 23:4)

Melchizedek Grips That Take You to Heaven
After moving to the Terrestrial Room and learning the Law of Chastity, we were taught the First Token of the Melchizedek Priesthood or Sign of the Nail, which, I was surprised to find, was quite similar to a handshake I had learned in Satanism. (See First Token of Melchizedek Priesthood Chart, p. 39). In witchcraft, this was the sign by which one Satanist could recognize

another.[35] Now I was being taught it as a way to make my way into the LDS Celestial Kingdom.

This First Melchizedek Priesthood grip is identical to the grip of the York Rite 9th degree—Knight of Malta—as well as the 8th degree Wiccan Sign of the Nail. And the *Second* Token of the Melchizedek Priesthood is very similar to the Real Grip of a Master Mason, which is called the Strong Grip of the Lion's Paw. In witchcraft, the Second Melchizedek grip is identical to the Strong Grip of the Lion of the Tribe of Judah.

What exactly do witches believe these grips achieve, beyond recognition signs? In witchcraft—and in the esoteric levels of European Masonry—I had learned that these strange grips were not just mummery. They had magickal effects on their practitioners. This was especially true of the grips used in the temple for the Melchizedek priesthood.

The essence of the Mormon temple ceremony is that you are learning *information (gnosis)* which you will use to get to heaven when you die. You will pass through a series of spiritual challenges which you will answer with passwords, signs and handshakes. Brigham Young made this public when he laid the cornerstone of the Salt Lake Temple:

> Your endowment is to receive all those ordinances in the House of the Lord, *which are necessary for you,* after you have departed this life, to enable you to walk back to the presence of the Father, *passing angels who stand as sentinels, being enabled to give them the key words, the sign and tokens..*"[35A]

In the temple, the grips and passwords eventually are all given to "The Lord—upon the Five Points of Fellowship".

Passing through the veil is symbolic of both resurrection and passing into paradise. In effect, these occult grips are supposed to have the *power* to raise you from death to eternal life.

In Masonry, the exact same thing is true. The initiation ceremony of a Master Mason includes a playlet in which the Grand Master Hiram Abiff is raised from death by "the brethren" who form a prayer circle and raise him by the Strong Grip of the Lion's Paw. They then (while standing in The Five Points of Fellowship) give him the secret Grand Masonic Word: MAH-HAH-BONE.

Witches, likewise, seek knowledge which will give them power over the natural elements and eventually over death itself. The highest magickal practices of witchcraft involve the working of alchemical changes in the body which will produce immortality. As a witch, I engaged in rituals designed to raise dead bodies to life through incantations, grips and other ritual.

Eastern Religious Connections

The grips of Mormonism, Magick and Masonry have their similarities in the Eastern Religions as well. One example is the 4000-year-old discipline of acupuncture (also practiced as *acupressure*).[36] This occult practice from China teaches that pressure on certain invisible lines of energy in the human body can cause physiological or even mental changes in the person. These lines are called meridians. (See pp. 45, 52-53)

The Sign of the Nail activates a point said in acupuncture to alleviate the symptoms of convulsions,

29

hiccoughs and insanity.[37] In the Craft this grip was regarded as powerful enough to stimulate the blind rage necessary to work real black magick.

The Second Token of the Melchizedek Priesthood, or Sure Sign of the Nail, applies pressure to a point on the meridian which pertains to sex and circulation.[38] The meridian runs up the right arm and over the shoulder, to arrive at the nipple—the precise anatomical spot where the Masonic square is stitched on the temple garment. (See 'Pressure Points" Chart, p. 45) The meridian travels down still further and terminates at the navel—the place where the *other* mark is stitched on the garment.[39]

The whole thing falls together incredibly well: the magickal marks on the garment are held together by a subtle occult web of sexual energy which is activated by pressure from the two highest grips in the LDS temple endowment!

The meridian activated by the Melchizedek grips is classified by the Chinese as Yang—fiery hot and masculine—which fits perfectly with the character of Lucifer as a solar-phallic god.

Applying pressure to the wrist in the Sure Sign of the Nail, or Patriarchal Grip, activates one of acupuncture's "Great Points."[40] A point considered to be tremendously powerful and versatile and is believed to have a profound impact on a person's psychosexual well-being (See "Pressure Points" Chart, p. 45). In the Craft, we were taught that this grip awakens latent sexual energies.

Witches even believe that it is possible, through magickal rites, to effect alchemical changes in their reproductive system to enable them to have viable relations with demon extraterrestrials. In the higher levels of witchcraft we were told that by having sex with these beings, spirit children could be brought into being.

In exchange for sex with us, the demons would bless us and our offspring with immortality and godhood.[41]

Mormonism, likewise, teaches that Jesus was begotten by just such a sexual union between an extraterrestrial god (The Mormon god Eloheim) and Mary.[42] Mormons believe that, as a result of the temple sealing rites, they can become gods and create spiritual offspring in order to populate their own worlds.

Before you dismiss these resemblances as too far-fetched, let me bring one thing to mind. I ask all people who have been through the temple to recall how very careful the temple workers are to make certain that the grips are done precisely. Consider how in the sealing ceremony, there is extreme care taken to make certain that the Patriarchal grip is right and that the cuff of the shirt does not prevent flesh from touching flesh. Recall how, in multiple proxy sealings, the man and woman are asked to make and break the patriarchal grip every time a new couple is brought up for the sealing; and how scrupulously careful the temple sealer is to be certain that the grip is always performed with proper contact. If there's nothing to this, then why are they so careful?

The Significance of "The Nail"
There is one more hellish connection with the grips—The Sign of the Nail and the Sure Sign of the Nail. Although it is a closely guarded secret among Luciferian, initiates, a code name for Satan is "The Nail." This is because nails caused so much pain to Jesus and because of their phallic symbolism. To find this title used in the LDS endowment surprised even me. It is a grisly association at best, especially in a religion which so

thoroughly rejects the cross. Satan fears the cross, but he loves being called The Nail.[43]

The "True Order of Prayer"

We were now ready to be taught "The True Order of Prayer." Here we gathered in a circle with the temple worker kneeling at the altar in the middle. We joined hands in the Patriarchal grip, alternating male and female.

There are still *more* correlations to witchcraft here. First of all, the overall arrangement is identical to the way Wiccan sabbaths are conducted. All covens meet in circles to do business, and the High Priestess' face is veiled. The witches in the circle hold hands in a grip nearly identical to what the Mormons call the Patriarchal Grip or Sure Sign of the Nail. The witches call it the Strong Grip of the Lion of the Tribe of Judah.[44] The High Priest or Priestess stands in the center and invokes the power of Lucifer or Diana or both.

The priests and priestesses of the coven even take care to alternate male/female, to establish the magickal polarity of witchcraft.[45] Magick can only flow well between man and woman.

Veiled Faces

At this point, just before passing through the veil into the Celestial Room of the temple, we pause to discuss the veiling of the women's faces, which has deep occult significance. An ancient and powerful archetype of the goddess of Wicca is Isis Veiled. Isis is the Egyptian name of the goddess of witchcraft. The Craft teaches that no man can see the face of Isis and live.[46] The Veiled Isis is custodian of the mysteries of darkness that must be veiled from the cowan (non-witch). In the occult, the Veiled Isis is man's only path to godhood. Why is she veiled? Because her face is too terrifying to behold; because the Mysteries of the magick she guards are awful; few, if any, can make it through the veil to the supernal triad of the Tree of Life, and hence godhood.[47]

The Mormon wife and the Wiccan High Priestess must each veil the face when in highest worship. The LDS wife, in a very real sense, is the gateway to godhood for her husband. In spite of all the LDS talk the patriarchal order, without the "mother in Zion", there will be no babies to magnify the husband's godhood. Sexuality is the key to the entire Mormon system. And, as the veil of the temple represents the doorway to the celestial kingdom, so the veil of the woman represents the doorway to exaltation.

The Veiled Isis is also the Consort of Lucifer. She is the keeper of the mysteries of sex and devil worship. Her veil is what keeps those who look into the mysteries from dying horribly. This is the real meaning of the veil that the LDS women must wear. It is an ancient fetish of a pagan priestesshood; and much of its horror cannot be written down for decent eyes.

Mormonism is, at its heart, a pagan fertility religion just like witchcraft. Veiling a woman destroys her identity as a person of value in the eyes of her Creator; and reduces her to an archetype; or worse, to her sexual attributes. It is what makes the temple endowment religious pornography. Sex, not Jesus, is at the heart of Mormonism (to which the ungodly practice of polygamy testifies). Veiled women belong in the temples of Lucifer in ancient Rome or in the harems of medieval Islam, not in a supposedly Christian temple.

Bottom line? The veil on the LDS wife's face symbolizes the "Mystery of Iniquity" (II Thes. 2:7),

Mystery Babylon the Great. (Rev. 17:5) It breaks my heart to say this, because I know most temple wives in Mormonism are striving to be good, virtuous women. They are sweet, beautiful people who have been drawn into an ever tightening web of occult rites and deception by men who should know better.

Paul's teaching in II Thessalonians, chapter two and the book of Colossians is clear: Mystery cults and Christianity stand in total opposition.

The Temple Veil

Speaking of veils, we are now at *the* veil of the LDS temple. This is the crowning moment of the endowment rite. Having been taught the "True Order of Prayer," we are next shown the Veil. This bears little resemblance to the veil of the temple of the Bible. It is a thin, gossamer kind of cloth with holes cut into it identical to the marks stitched on the temple garment, only larger. This veil is where we will go to have our knowledge of all the secret words and grips tested in a ritual similar to the central teaching of the *Tibetan Book of the Dead*.

We clasp hands through the holes in the veil with a temple worker on the other side who represents the Mormon god. Then a little catechism proceeds of sign/countersign which is quite identical to Masonic practice.[48] A veil worker is present to be certain that we get all the grips and words precisely right—especially the first-timers.

Since I had on a pink tag indicating I was a first-timer, my veil worker was especially pleased to see how well I knew all the tokens. He probably thought I was especially spiritual. *I didn't have the heart to tell him that I'd learned all of them already in witchcraft rites. And I'm sure he wouldn't have believed me.*

The final name of the Melchizedek priesthood is only given "through the veil, on the Five Points of Fellowship." This is a term used in both Masonry and witchcraft. In Masonry, its meaning and execution are identical to the temple rite, except there is no veil. In Druidic Wicca, the meaning and execution are also identical, but in other rites of Wicca, the meaning and execution are more sexually explicit.[49]

We embrace through the veil on the Five Points, and I received the highest secret of the endowment whispered into my right ear. This is just like all real occult secrets. True magickal secrets are never supposed to be written down, but only communicated orally. They are passed down by word of mouth from initiator to initiate. This is why some of these occult "secrets" mentioned in this piece are so difficult to document; because they are regarded so highly that they are never committed to paper!

American Masonry has vestiges of this in that they do not allow their ritual monitors to be printed except in a cipher and the ultimate secret of Blue Lodge Masonry is communicated exactly like the temple secret: orally and in low breath on the Five Points of Fellowship.

In any event, this "Second Name of the Melchizedek Priesthood" was given me by the worker on the other side of the veil. I found it was virtually a verbatim copy of a blessing that the pontiff of Satan gives his followers after the black mass. Here I was, at the pinnacle of LDS sanctity, and I was hearing a Satanic invocation! Here is the Satanic version:

> "May you have health in the navel and marrow in the bones, strength in your ***** and in your sinews; and power in the

priesthood be upon you and upon your posterity through all generations of time and throughout all eternity. Selah!"

And here is the LDS temple version:

"Health in the navel, marrow in the bones, strength in the loins and in the sinews, power in the Priesthood be upon me and upon my posterity through all generations of time and throughout all eternity."

This invocation seals the Satanic bondage of the temple endowment upon the temple patron's children and even grandchildren. Note that there is not a meaningful whit of difference between the Satanic blessing and the temple token, even though this token is supposed to be the highest blessing available to a Mormon in this life.[50]

If this seems unbelievable, just look at the content of this "sacred" invocation: "health…strength…power…" Nothing there that would offend a witch. Where are the Christian virtues: charity, faith, hope? The fruit of the Spirit?

Face it, this is a pagan prayer. Nowhere is Jesus, salvation, or heaven even mentioned. Just the same destiny that witches believe await them: eternal power, celestial sex, and spiritual evolution on a never-ending ego trip. The way of the world is Manipulation, Seduction, and Power; Christianity is the way of Sacrifice, Submission, and Service.

After being drawn through the veil by the Patriarchal grip, we were all led into the Celestial Room—a huge, airy room looking like a lush hotel lobby done in off-

First Token of the Aaronic Priesthood

Mormonism	Magick/Masonry

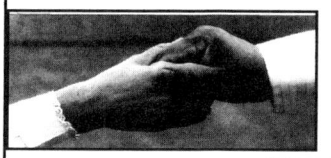

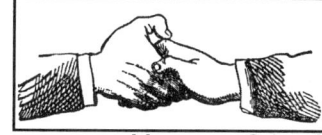

Token or Grip

Masonry: Grip of Entered Apprentice *(Duncans Ritual, p. 36)*

Name

Mormonism: New Secret Temple Name

Masonry: "Boaz"
Witchcraft: New Secret Craft Name

Sign and Execution of Penalty

Obligation and Penalty of an Entered Apprentice Mason: "I will…ever conceal and never reveal, any arts, parts or points of the hidden mysteries…under no less penalty than that of having my throat cut across, my tongue torn out by its roots, and my body buried in the rough sands of the sea…" *(Duncan's Ritual, pp.34-35)*

Masonry: Sign of Entered Apprentice *(Duncans Ritual, p. 17)*

"The penalty is executed by placing the right thumb under the left ear, palm down, fingers close together, the thumb is drawn quickly across the throat to the right ear…" *(Mormon Temple Ceremony)*

Second Token of the Aaronic Priesthood

Mormonism   Magick/Masonry

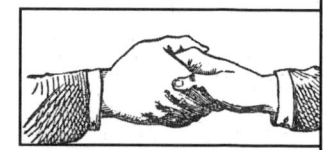

Token or Grip

Masonry: Grip of a Fellow Craft Mason *(Duncans Ritual,* p. 66) Witchcraft 3°, "Sign of Pan"

Name

Mormonism: Your own First (Given) Name

Masonry: "Jachin"
Witchcraft: New Secret Craft Name

Sign and Execution of Penalty

Obligation and penalty of a Fellow Craft Mason: "I will…ever conceal, and never reveal any of the secret, arts, parts, or points of the Fellow Craft Degree…binding myself under no less penalty than of having my breast torn open, my heart plucked out and placed on the highest pinnacle of the temple." *(Duncan's Ritual,* pp. 64 & 65).

"**The penalty is executed by placing the right hand on the left breast, and drawing the hand quickly accros the chest…**" *(Mormon Temple Ceremony)*

Masonry: Sign of a Fellow Craft Mason *(Duncans Ritual,* p. 17)

First Token of the Melchizedek Priesthood
or Sign of the Nail

Mormonism   Magick/Masonry

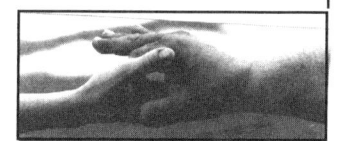

Token or Grip

Masonry: Ninth Degree, York Rite, "Knight of Malta"
Witchcraft 8°, "Sign of the Nail"

Name

Mormonism: "The Son" formerly "The Sun"

Magick: Your name (motto) as a "god"

Sign and Execution of Penalty

Obligation and penalty of a Master Mason: "I will…ever conceal, and never reveal any of the secret, arts, parts, or points of the Master Degree… binding myself under no less penalty than that of having my body severed in two, my bowels taken from thence and burned to ashes, the ashes scattered before the four winds..." *(Duncan's Ritual, pp. 64 & 65)*

"The right thumb is placed over the left hip, the left hand is held in a cupping position. The penalty is executed by drawing the thumb quickly across the body…." *(Mormon Temple Ceremony)*

Sign of a Master Mason *(Duncans Ritual, p. 18)*

39

Second Token of the Melchizedek Priesthood...

Mormonism

Grip

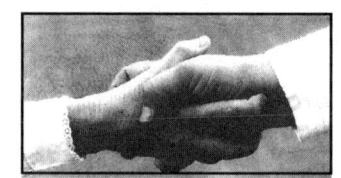

Mormonism: Patriarchal Grip or Sure Sign of the Nail

Name

An incantation done on the "Five Points of Fellowship"

Mormon Incantation

"Health in the navel, marrow in the bones, strength in the loins and in the sinews, power in the Priesthood be upon me and upon my posterity through all generations of time and throughout all eternity."

Mormonism's "Five Points"

1. Inside of right foot by side of right foot.
2. Knee to knee.
3. Breast to breast.
4. Hand to back.
5. Mouth to ear.
(Temple Ceremony)

Sign - Penalty

Mormonism's sign is made by raising both hands high above the head and while lowering the hands chanting:
"Pay Lay Ale"
"Pay Lay Ale"
"Pay Lay Ale"

Mormonism's Penalty
"No penalty is mentioned"

...the Patriarchal Grip or Sure Sign of the Nail

Masonry

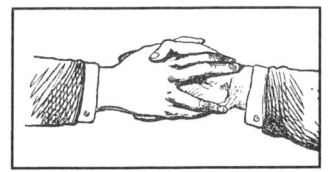

Masonry: Real Grip of a Master Mason
(*Duncan's Ritual,* p. 120)

Magick

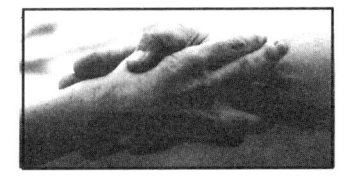

Witchcraft: The Strong Grip of the Lion of the Tribe of Judah

Masonry's "Five Points of Fellowship" (*Duncan's Ritual,* p. 121). Foot to foot, knee to knee, breast to breast, hand to back, and cheek, or mouth, to ear.'

Magick Incantation

"Health in the navel, marrow in the bones, strength in the...and in the sinews, power in the Priesthood be upon me and upon my posterity through all generations of time and throughout all eternity."

Masonic Penalty

"...I most solemnly, sincerely promise and swear...binding myself under no less penalty than that of having my body severed in two, my bowels taken from thence and burned to ashes, the ashes scattered before the four winds of heaven...should I ever, nowingly, violate this my Master Mason's obligation." (*Duncan's Ritual,* p. 96)

Grand Hailing Sign of a Master Mason (*Duncan's Ritual,* p. 18)

The Three Temples

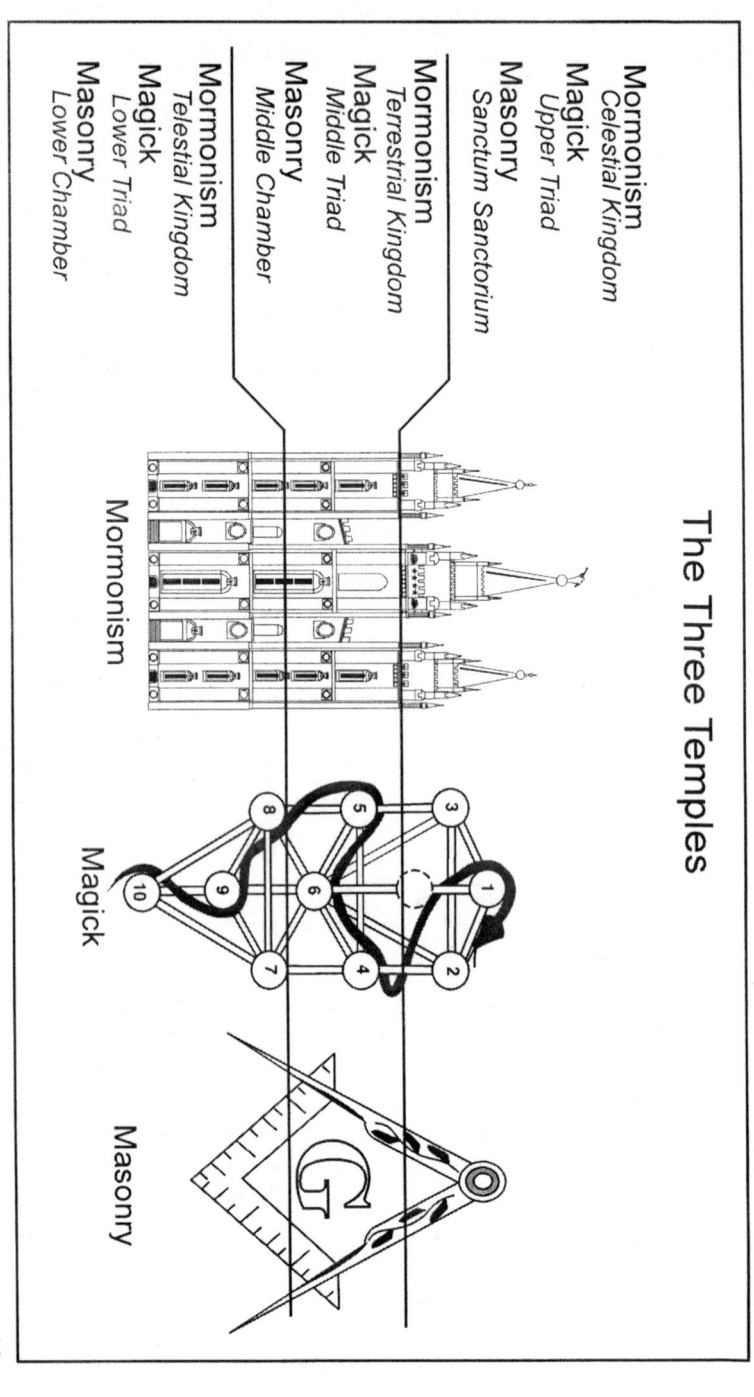

Mormonism
Celestial Kingdom
Magick
Upper Triad
Masonry
Sanctum Sanctorium

Mormonism
Terrestrial Kingdom
Magick
Middle Triad
Masonry
Middle Chamber

Mormonism
Telestial Kingdom
Magick
Lower Triad
Masonry
Lower Chamber

Mormonism

Magick

Masonry

Fifteen Ceremonial Similarities

Mormonism	Masonry	Magick
1. Stripped of clothing	Stripped & divested of metal	Stripped & divested of metal
2. Dressed in white shield	Dressed in blue pajamas, left breast bare	Dressed in black shield
3. Washed, anointed and sealed	Appointed in Melchizedek Priesthood (19° Scottish Rite)	Anointed & sealed
4. Given temple garment for protection	Given apron to justify Mason at Great White Throne	Taught use and wearing of talismatic garments
5. Get "New Name"		Get "Craft" name
6. Creation room narrative circumambulation originally in the Temple	Circumambulation of lodge room symbolizing chaos before creation	Initiate Circumambulates Magick Circle
7. Put on apron	Receive apron	3° initiate receives apron
8. Covenants: Law of obedience Law of sacrifice	1° obligattion	1° oath of obedience
9. Clothed in robes of the holy priesthood (robe, cap, or veil, & sash—girdle)	Vested in Melchizdek Priesthood robes 19° Scottish Rite	Vested in Melchizedek Priesthood robes 5°
10. Grips	Grips	Grips
11. Prayer circle	⎣——— Identical ———⎦	Prayer Circle
12. Veil Lecture	Masonic attributes of veil sign ⎣—— Identical ——⎦	Magick attributes of veil sign
13. Veil Challenges ⎣—— Identical ——⎦	Masonic Challenges	
14. Five Points of Fellowship	Conveying of 3° word at the grave of Hiram Abif	Five Points of Fellowship 3°
15. Name of 2nd Token of Melchizedek Preisthood ⎣——— Identical (except one word) ———⎦		Santanic blessing 6° and above
Celestial Room & Godhood	Sanctum sanctorium & Godhood	10° Ipssissmus (Godhood)

The Tree of Life

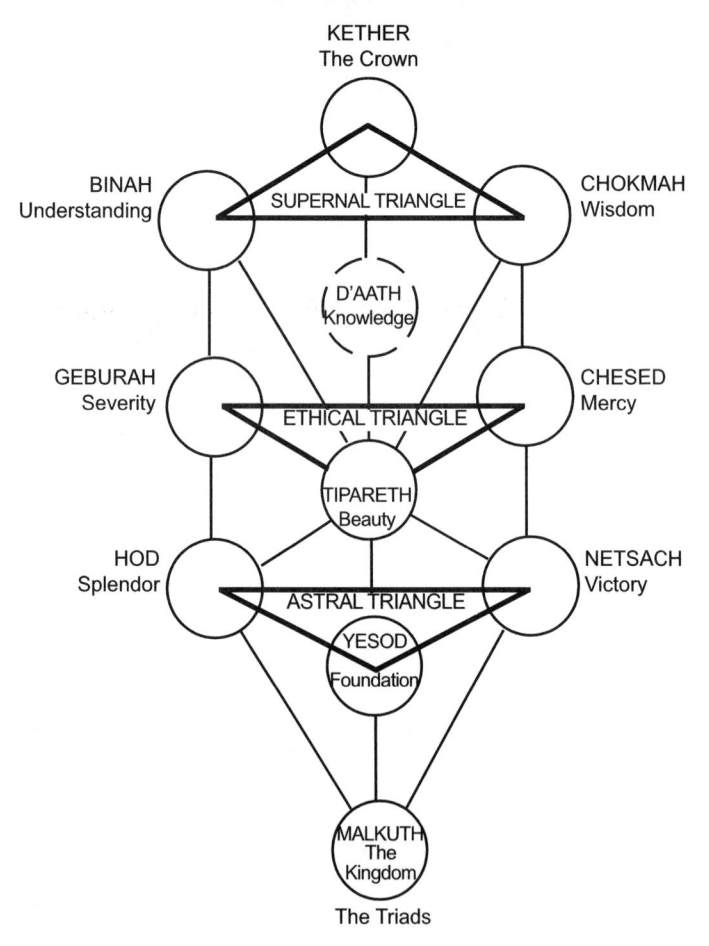

```
                        KETHER
                      The Crown
                          ○
                       ╱─────╲
              BINAH  ╱SUPERNAL╲  CHOKMAH
          Understanding TRIANGLE  Wisdom
                ○    ╲─────────╱   ○
                      ╲  D'AATH ╱
                       Knowledge
                       
            GEBURAH                CHESED
            Severity  ETHICAL      Mercy
                ○    TRIANGLE       ○
                      TIPARETH
                       Beauty
                       
              HOD                  NETSACH
            Splendor  ASTRAL       Victory
                ○    TRIANGLE       ○
                       YESOD
                     Foundation
                     
                      MALKUTH
                       The
                      Kingdom
```

The Triads

In witchcraft, as in Mormonism and Masonry, "Eternal Progression" is based on advancing in knowledge. One progresses in occult knowledge as the various levels of the Tree of Life are "manifested." The Tree may be used as a method of visulization and meditation, as a structure for Tarot Card reading, and as a source of knowledge through correct pronunciation of the Hebrew names.

"The primary glyph or mandala of the Qabalah—and so of the Western (Esoteric) Tradition also—is the Tree of Life, which is the 'roadmap'...the Tarot and the Tree form a route to mystical illumination and magical power...[and are] a means of achieving union with Godhead..." (Emily Peach, *The Tarot Workbook,* The Aquarian Press, Wellingborough, Northamptonshire, England, 1984, pp. 180 and 226)

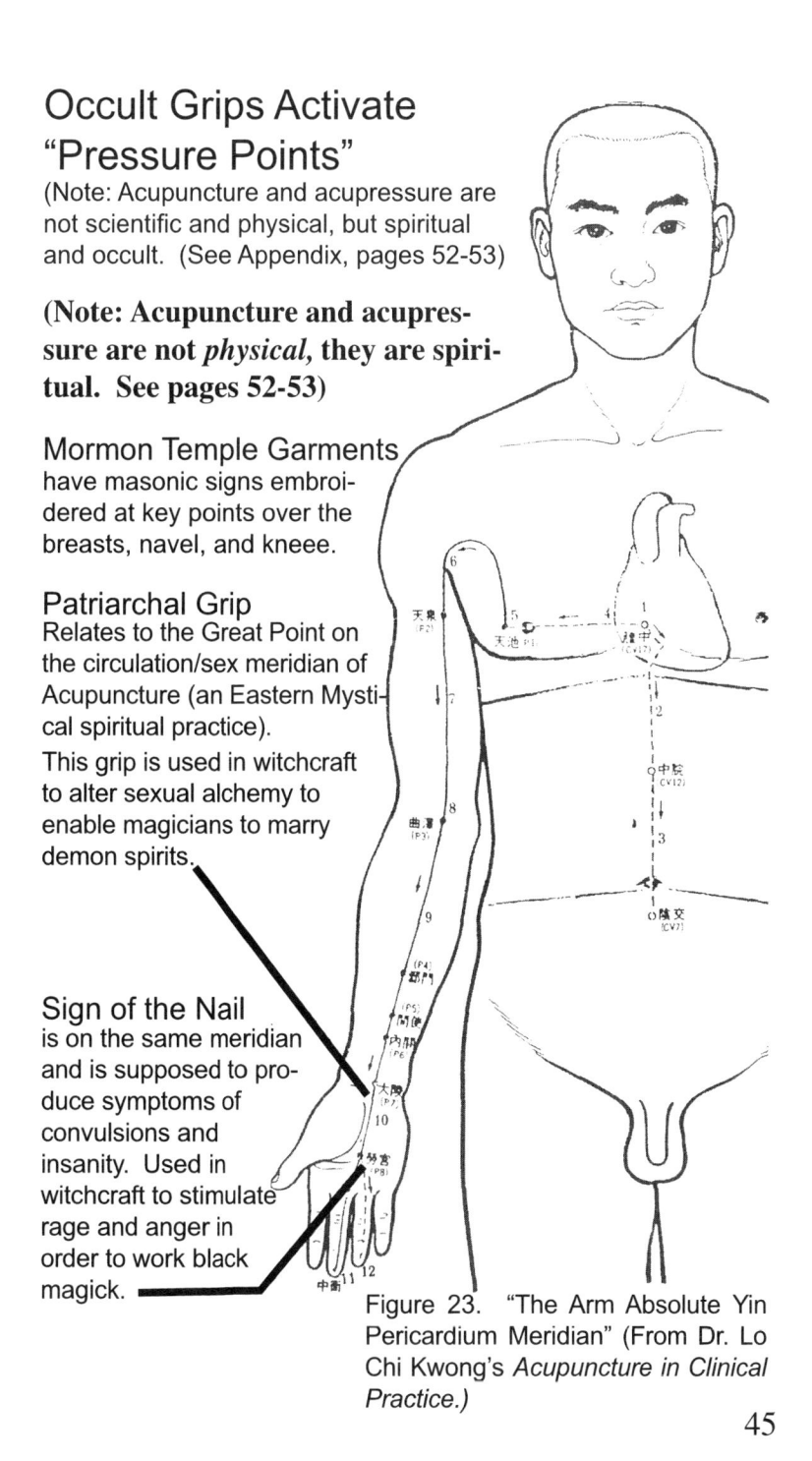

Occult Grips Activate "Pressure Points"
(Note: Acupuncture and acupressure are not scientific and physical, but spiritual and occult. (See Appendix, pages 52-53)

(Note: Acupuncture and acupressure are not *physical*, they are spiritual. See pages 52-53)

Mormon Temple Garments
have masonic signs embroidered at key points over the breasts, navel, and kneee.

Patriarchal Grip
Relates to the Great Point on the circulation/sex meridian of Acupuncture (an Eastern Mystical spiritual practice).

This grip is used in witchcraft to alter sexual alchemy to enable magicians to marry demon spirits.

Sign of the Nail
is on the same meridian and is supposed to produce symptoms of convulsions and insanity. Used in witchcraft to stimulate rage and anger in order to work black magick.

Figure 23. "The Arm Absolute Yin Pericardium Meridian" (From Dr. Lo Chi Kwong's *Acupuncture in Clinical Practice.*)

45

whites. This represents the Celestial Kingdom, the goal of every devout Mormon.

If you were to be married, you would be ushered upstairs for your sealing. The sealing allegedly seals you and your mate together for time and all eternity in heaven (contrary to Jesus teaching in Luke 20:35). It is also similar in many respects to the wedding, called a handfasting, which my wife and I had undergone in 1973. Then we were in a forest clearing near Zion State Park north of Chicago and were surrounded by almost 200 witches.

Temple Architecture
The temple buildings, as well as the rituals are similar in Mormonism, Magick and Masonry. The cross, for example, is conspicuously absent from all LDS temples. And the older temples are literally festooned with occult and Masonic markings. On the Salt Lake temple alone are:

1) All-seeing eye—an eye in a triangle surrounded by rays of light—like an ancient Egyptian symbol of Heru-paar-Kraat, the Widget Eye. Heru was the hawk-headed lord of Satanic power.

2) Masonic handshakes.

3) Suns—symbols of the ancient sungod, Ba'al, the arch rival of the true Biblical God, Yahweh (I Kings 18 and elsewhere).

4) Moon phases—symbols of the witch goddess, Diana or Artemis, the queen of heaven. The dark phases of the Moon are for black magick, the full phases of the Moon for white magick.

5) Upright pentagrams (5-pointed star)—the universal symbol of witchcraft and the goddess. It's richness in meaning is far too lengthy to detail here. Suffice it to say

that there is no single symbol more associated with magick.

6) Big Dipper constellation (Usra Major)—all constellations have magickal significance. This one was sacred to the ancient Egyptian worship of Set (the Egyptian god of evil) and was used by Sets votaries to determine the time of his ascendancy.

7) Inverted pentagrams (single point down)—universally regarded as an evil symbol, many witches will not use it because it is used to call down the power of Satan![51] (also found on the Logan temple.) Eleven large inverted pentagrams decorated the (original) Nauvoo Temple.[51A]

8) Hexagram—(6-pointed star within a circle) though sometimes associated with Judaism, this star, when within a circle, is the symbol of anti-Christ. It has 6 points, 6 angles, and an interior polygon of 6 sides—hence the perfect symbol of 666. Though I have not found this on the Salt Lake Temple, it is right across the park, emblazoned all over the Assembly Hall. And it exists in a stronger form on the Logan temple: inverted with two points up.

Numbers 1, 2, 6, 7, and 8 are very sinister symbols. And they were included, not by accident, but by intent. Brigham Young, who claimed he got the design for the Salt Lake Temple "by revelation", incorporated occult designs on the structure's stone surface:

> "Brigham Young…made provisions in the original plans for the temple to incorporate numerous symbols that functioned with medieval complexity to speak of the order of God…"[51B]

As a matter of fact, Young's original plans called for markings that were too complex to execute in the granite walls of the temple:

> "In 1870, Truman Angel made major revisions in the plans for the exterior of the temple with removal or alterations of many symbolic motifs. (Brigham Young was responsible for the revisions because of the change in building material from adobe and freestone to granite; granite could not accept the fine detail required by many of the symbols.) The *Saturn-stones* were eliminated...the *faces of the sun-stones and moon-stones*...were either simplified or removed."[51C]

The Church leaders called upon one of its great intellects to make sure the temple was astrologically aligned:

> "In 1878, a plan of the Temple's exterior walls was purposely drafted to plot the exact location of each of the fifty moonstones according to lunar phase, month and year. *This was determined by observations made that year in anticipation of the next season's building program when the moonstones were to be laid.* The individual most capable of such an observation was Orson Pratt...In 1869, an astronomical observatory of wood and adobe was constructed specifically for him on the

southeast corner of the Temple Block…"[51D]

The inclusion of all this symbolism is especially ironic when one considers how the Mormon Church reacts with almost vampiric revulsion to the cross of Jesus Christ. What kind of Christian church spurns the cross and then covers its building with magick symbols?

Remember, Paul counseled his saints to avoid even the appearance of evil (I Thes. 5:22). Evil symbols decorate the LDS temples; and the ceremonies within are festering cankers of Satanism. No wonder so many LDS never return to the temple. The very Spirit of the Living God cries out from within them: "Unclean! Unclean!"

Occult symbols, in and of themselves, are not always totally incriminating. But when you find such a large number of these symbols—many of them really evil—the evidence begins to mount. I cannot find any other place where the inverted pentagram is used outside Satanism. It is just too evil a sign—it draws demons!

When you examine Mormon temple architecture in the light (or, rather the darkness) of the ceremonies performed within the temples walls, the symbols begin to tell a fearful tale. Believe me, the Mormon people have every right to get nervous about their temples. They are a Chinese puzzlebox of evil. Open up the exterior architecture of the temple and you find witchcraft symbols. Look inside that box and you find ceremonies rich in occult and Satanic meaning and phrases. You discover that the temple is predicated upon an occult/gnostic philosophy which is thoroughly congenial to witches, Satanists, and members of the "New Age Movement."

49

All these occult groups believe that people can evolve into gods or goddesses.[52] They all believe in the LDS doctrine of "eternal progression." So did the ancient heretics, the gnostics.[53] The essential principle that man is God is the very cornerstone of occult philosophy. It reflects the so-called Hermetic Maxim: "As above, so below!"[54]

Just as in the temple, these secrets are too "sacred" to be written down. They can only be communicated from mouth to ear. This is the very meaning of the word Qabalah.[55] But nowhere does Jesus discuss secrets or arcane knowledge. Quite the contrary, He proclaimed:

> "I have spoken openly to the world...I always taught in the synagogues or at the temple, where all the Jews come together. *I have said nothing in secret."* (John 18.20)

Why, in the light of Jesus' dedication to openness and transparency, does the Mormon Church continue to perpetuate—among trusting people—all these "sacred secrets?"

It is my prayer that by exposing the real roots of the temple ceremony, I will make it easier for my LDS friends to decide in whom they are going to place their eternal trust.

Will it be in the pure light of the gospel of Jesus Christ, or in the dark, dull shadows of Joseph Smith and Mormonism's Temple of Doom?

The End

Renouncing Evil

What you have just read may have struck home personally for you. Perhaps you have been involved in Mormonism, Magick or Masonry (or some other occult organization or practice). If that is so, we recommend that you take time right now to pray for deliverance.

The Bible states: "resist the Devil and he will flee from you." If you are not a Christian if your do not know for sure that you are saved then you need to pray the following prayer:

> *"Lord Jesus, I confess that I am a sinner who stands in need of deliverance from the power of evil. I ask you to forgive my sins and wash me with your blood. I want you to be the only Lord of my life. Make me your disciple."*

Next, you need to contact a Bible-believing church and make an appointment with the pastor. Tell him where you are coming from and that you need spiritual grounding.

If you are a Christian, but have been involved with any area of the occult, you need to renounce the activity and pray for deliverance.

Acupuncture

(From *Hard Case Witnessing: Winning "Impossibles" for Christ,* James R. Spencer, Chosen Books, 1991)

What is acupuncture? Most Americans have heard of it. Many have received acupuncture treatment for a variety of ailments, or to help stop smoking or lose weight. The people I ask generally assume it has something to do with the nervous system: A needle is inserted into a nerve pathway, which interrupts pain or alters the flow of electro-chemical energy. That, however, is **not** what acupuncture is. Let's hear it from an acupuncturist, Dr. Ruth Lever, author of *Acupuncture for Everyone:*

> Acupuncture…is a single therapy, using the insertion of needles into the skin to treat a variety of ailments which might be treated by Western doctors with drugs or surgery…The reason it is able to treat all ailments in the same way is because it sees them as stemming from the same cause—*a disruption to the energy flow or vital force of the body* (p. 11).

Well, our first question should be: "What *is* the vital force that acupuncture interrupts?" Dr. Lever confirms that it is the Oriental concept of *Chi* (pronounced chee):

The Chinese see the whole functioning of the body and mind as being dependent on the normal flow of body energy, or life force, which they call Chi (pp. 42—43). Chi, Dr. Lever says, is a "universal energy which surrounds and pervades everything." Furthermore, "My Chi is not distinct from your Chi." Chi is like light energy or radio waves, *but it cannot be seen or felt. And it does not disappear at death:* "There is a constant interchange between the Chi of the body and the Chi of the environment" (p. 43).

Lever says the Chi force is related to the Eastern concept of Yin and Yang. Chi circulates throughout the body along "meridians." These meridians *cannot be located physically, nor identified electronically.* The description of the vital force of the body sounds very much like the soul or the spirit. In fact, the Oriental originators of acupuncture declared Chi to be the spiritual essence of not only the body, but the universe.

It is obvious that the simplest exploration of acupuncture demonstrates that it is a *spiritual,* not a *physical* phenomenon. If it is a spiritual phenomenon, where is the Scripture sanctioning it? Where is the protection of the blood of Christ in it?

Those involved in acupuncture are involved in spiritual manipulation of the body. That is the essence of the occult. There is not, in acupuncture, even the pretense of legitimate science.

Many people ask about *acupressure.* (or reflexology) It is precisely the same as acupuncture without the needles, using the same spiritual "meridians."

Footnotes

1. From a private document available by request from the author.

2. Ibid. See also the writings of such theosophical writers as Helena Blavatsky and Elizabeth C. Prophet for copious references to the "White Brotherhood."

2A. Manly P. Hall, the great arcane lexicographer in his *The Secret Teachings of All Ages,* says:
> "all forms of...magic are but blind alleys...those who...wander therein almost invariably fall victim to their imprudence. Man, incapable of controlling his own appetites, is not equal to the task of governing the fiery and tempestuous elemental spirits.
> "Many a magician has lost his life as the result of opening a way whereby submundane creatures could become active participants in his affairs." *The Secret Teachings of All Ages,* "Ceremonial Magic and Sorcery", The Philosophical Research Society, 1971.

3. From a private document available from the author upon request. See also Allegro, John, *The Sacred Mushroom and the Cross,* Doubleday & Co., 1970. Although the book is astonishingly reductionist in its approach to Christianity, he does document the use of anointing and similar practices thoroughly among ancient peoples.

4. Farrar, Stewart, *What Witches Do,* Coward, McCann, and Geoghegan, New York, 1971, p. 93. (Quoting Alexandrian/Gardnerian Rite *Book of Shadows).*

5. Duncan, Malcom C., *Masonic Ritual and Monitor* (otherwise cited as *Duncan's Ritual Monitor),* David McKay Co., New York, p. 30

6. Gray, William S., *The Office of the Holy Tree of Life,* Sangreal, 1970, P. 16-17; Regardie, Israel, *The Golden Dawn,* Llewellyn, 1971, p.122 (2 volume set)

7. Grey, pp. 14-15

8. Duncan, p.61

9. Qabalah is a system of Jewish mysticism of baffling antiquity. It seems to have begun in the Creation mysticism which surrounded Genesis 1. This may have later fused with the Merkabah ("Throne of Glory") school of Hebrew mysticism which based itself on Ezk. 1 and then been swamped by the heresies of Jewish gnosticism. It was first written down in the Middle East (c.300-600) in the *Sefer Yetzirah,* or "Book of Creation." After many changes, it became thoroughly polluted with medieval occultism and Rosicrucianism, until the 17th century, when it became the groundplan for virtually all magickal societies. See Scholem, Gershom G., *Major Trends in Jewish Mysticism,* Schocken Books; or Regardie, Israel, *The Tree of Life,* Samuel Weiser, 1983.

10. Achad, Frater, *The Anatomy of the Body of God,* Samuel Weiser, 1973, esp. p. 41.

11. To thoroughly address the subject of Masonic symbols and their relation to the occult would be well beyond the scope of this article. Those interested may wish to read, "Freemasonry, Satan's Flytrap", by the author, available through One Accord Ministries, Box 457, Dubuque, IA 52004.

12. Frost, Gavin, "Witchcraft, the Way to Serenity", School of Wicca, 1978, p. 1.

13. Mathers, S.L. MacGregor, *The Greater Key of Solomon,* DeLaurence and Co., Chicago, 1914 edited from British Museum Sloane MSS. 1307, 3091; Add. MSS. 10, 862; Harleian MSS. 3981; King's MSS., 288 and

Lansdown MSS., 1202 and 1203—seven codices in all. The museum dates these documents back to the *1590's.* See especially p. 95 in the DeLaurence edition. These markings are the exact same concept as the stitchings on the Mormon temple garments.)

14. Heckethorn, Charles W., *The Secret Societies of All Ages and Countries,* University Books, Inc. Hyde Park, NY, 1965, v.2, p. 11)

15. Durham, Reed C., *No Help for the Widow's Son* Martin Publishing Co., Nauvoo, Il, 1980, p. 25

16. Ibid., pp. 15-17

17. Smith, Joseph, Jr., *History of the Church,* The Church of Jesus Christ of Latter-day Saints, v. 4, p. 552

18. Ibid., v. 5, pp. 1-2.

18A. Duncan, p. 121, fig. 18.

19. Goodwin, S.H., *Mormonism and Masonry,* Masonic Service Assn. of the United States, Washington D.C., 1924 pp. 56-64

20. Frazer, Sir James, *The New Golden Bough,* (ed. by Dr. Theodore Gaster, Criterion, 1959, p. 187; also, *Man, Myth, and Magic,* pp.1940-41.

21. The second "prophet" of Mormonism, Brigham Young. firmly and irrevocably taught that Adam was actually God: *Journal of Discourses,* v. 1, pp. 50-51; "Millennial Star," v15, p. 801, 825; v. 16, p. 530. Today the Mormon Church publicly denies the doctrine was ever taught.

21A. Sackett, Chuck, *What's Going On In There,* Sword of the Shepherd Ministries, Inc., Thousand Oaks, CA, pp. 7-8

22. Rudolf, Kurt, *Gnosis,* T. J. Clark, 1983, pp 81-82.

23. Brown, Harold, O. J., *Heresies,* Doubleday and Co., New York, 1984, p. 254-255.

24. *Man, Myth, and Magic,* vol. 17, p. 2338; Runciman, Steve, *The Medieval Manichee,* Cambridge, UK, 1946, p. 97.

24A. Farrar, p. 26.

25. Sackett, p. 27.

26. *Deseret News,* Church Section, July 31, 1965, p. 7

27. Smith, Joseph Fielding, *Doctrines of Salvation,* v. 1, p. 114-115; see also LDS scripture, "Pearl of Great Price," Moses 5:10-11.

28. Crowley, Alesiter, 777, privately printed by *The OTO* 1907, p. 13; also *Duncan's Ritual Monitor,* 39. For Rosicrucians, see AMORC's member's catalog for a picture of the Rosicrucian apron in full color: AMORC, San Jose, CA; also private document from grimoire available from the author.

29. Kundalini is the controlled force of sexual, serpent energy that yogis believe is coiled at the base of the spine in the Muladhara chakra. Douglas and Singer, *Sexual Secrets,* Destiny Books, New York, 1979, pp. 43-46, 71-72, 182. (It's quite "adult" reading though!)

30. Crowley, pp. 7,11.

31. Many Bible scholars feel that John 1:1-14 is partially an anti-gnostic polemic, in that it stresses: a) that Jesus is the Eternal *Logos*, the Word; and b) that this *Logos* became flesh (Gr. *Sarx).* Scholars also identify I Tim. 6:20 and I Cor. 2:10 as possible attacks on gnostic heresy by Paul; as

well as Rev. 2:24. The "Colossian Heresy" may well have been a form of Jewish gnosticism. Among the early fathers who condemned the doctrine were Irenaeus *(Against Heresies);* Clement of Alexandria *(Stromata,* c. 215), and Tertullian *(Against Marcion* and *Against Valentinus,* c. 220).

32. For gnostic texts of Lucifer teaching Eve, see *The Nag Hammadi Codicies;* II, 5, 113 (161) 21-114 (162) 2.

32A. Albert Pike, "Instructions to the Twenty-Three Supreme Councils of the World", as quoted in *The Question of Freemasonry,* J. Edward Decker, Free the Masons Ministries, P.O. Box 1977, Issaquah, WA., 98027, p. 13.

33. See Brigham's comments about the fate of "covenan breakers," if you doubt the oaths were taken seriously: *Journal of Discourses,* The Church of Jesus Christ of Latter-day Saints, Vol. 3, p. 247; J. M. Grant, Vol. 4, p. *50.* See also: Spencer, James R., *Have You Witnessed to a Mormon Lately?,* Spencer Books, Box 8656, Boise, ID 83707, pp.148-151.

34. Duncan, p. 18, fig. 7.

35. This grip also happens to be the grip of the Knights of Malta degree in the York Rite, a preparatory degree to the sinister Knights Templar degree. *(Richardson's Monitor,* p. 126)

35A. Hamilton, C. Mark and Cutrubus, C. Nina, *The Salt Lake Temple: A Monument to a People,* University Services Salt Lake City, 1983, p.141.

36. Kwong, Lo Chi, *Acupuncture in Clinical Practice* Comercial Press Ltd., Hong Kong, 1979, p. 1; Koch, Kurt, *Occult ABC,* Literature Mission Aglasterhausen Inc., Germany (distributed by Grand Rapids Internationa Publications, P.O.Box 2607, Grand Rapids, MI, pp.5-11.)

37. Kwong, p. 66.

38. Thie, John F., D.C., *Touch for Health,* deVros and Co., Marina del Rey, CA. 1979, pp. 70-77; also Austin, Dr. Mary, *The Textbook of Acupuncture Therapy,* ASI Publ., New York, 1978, pp. 43-47.

39. Kwong, p. 68-69.

40. Austin, p. 44.

41. This is, of course, the sort of gross, necromantic practice which may well have been one of the main reasons why God destroyed the world through the flood! (See Gen. 6:2-7) Naturally we were taught that the "sons of God" in v. 2 were the extraterrestrial demon spirits with whom we were dealing. We were also taught that the Nephilim (the Hebrew word usually translated "giants" in v. 4) were the spirit children like those we would try to conceive—godlike beings who would help bring forth the New Age of Enlightenment.

42. Many LDS prophets and authorities have taught that the Mormon god Elohim had relations with Mary to conceive Jesus. See MeConkie, Bruce R., *Mormon Doctrine,* p. 742; *Journal of Discourses,* v.8, p. 115; v.1, p. 50-51; v.11, p. 268; and Smith, Joseph Fielding, *Doctrines of Salvation,* v.1, pp. 18-19.

43. A "code word", by its nature, is zealously guarded, even as Masonic secrets were guarded a couple of centuries ago. One who betrays these secrets suffers horribly. This is why many Satanists were stunned to find the use of the word "Nail" in its correct context in the third "Omen" movie, "The Final Conflict," coming from the mouth of the actor playing the son of Satan. These films were carefully researched and used authentic Satanic music and rites, but the use of "the nail" was unprecedented. See McGill, Gord, *The Final Conflict,* Signet, 1980, p. 81-82.

44. From a private document available from the author.

45. Farrar, pp. 20, 26.

46. This is not a parody of I Tim. 6:16 exactly. It refers to the rite of the Divine King in which the High Priest of a coven is slain during the Great Rite after looking upon the unveiled face of the goddess, that the land might be nurished with his blood. This is still done in a few raditional covens, especially during the times of poor crops James Frazer speaks of this extensively in *The Golden Bough.*

47. Farrar, pp. 121, 128; also Crowley, *The Book of Thoth,* Samuel Weiser, 1971, p. 72-74.

48. Duncan, p. 37, for instance.

49. Farrar, p. 94: "five are the points of fellowship...' quoting from the 3rd degree sexual initiation, the Great Rite; see also Duncan, p. 121, fig. 18, for the Masonic version; and author's private document on Druidic five points of fellowship.

50. From private documents available from the author.

51. Hartmann, Dr. Franz, *Magic: White and Black,* pp 290-291; also see *Man, Myth and Magic,* v. 16, p. 2159 and the cover of *The Satanic Bible,* Lavey, Anton Szandor, Avon, 1969.

51A. Hamilton and Cuturbus, p. 44.

51B. Hamilton and Cuturbus, p. 142.

51C. Hamilton and Cuturbus, p. 54.

51D. Hamilton and Cuturbus, p. 142-143.

52. Adler, Margot, *Drawing Down the Moon,* Beacon Press, Boston, 1979, P. *25;* and Russell, Jeffrey, *A History of Witchcraft,* Thames & Hudson, Ltd., London, 1980, pp. 46-51, pp. 158-159.

53. Rudolph, p. 92-93 for a direct relationship between ancient Gnosticism and the doctrine of eternal progression.

54. The Hermetic Maxim is from an emerald tablet in Egypt, engraved by the mythic Magi, Hermes Trismegistus. It forms the central lynchpin of occultism: The idea that man and God are just quantitatively different; and that a man, through his own discipline and rigorous training can become a god. For a complete transcription of the Hermetic Maxim, see *Zolar's Encyclopedia of Ancient and Forbidden Knowledge,* Arco Publ., New York, 1970, p. 114.

55. *Man, Myth and Magic,* v. 3, p. 282. Also Grey, *Concepts of Qabalah,* Weiser, 1984, p. 13.

Chronology of William Schoebelen

09/22/68 1st Degree (Gardnerian Tradition) Witch
09/01/70 2nd Degree
05/15/71 Bachelor's Degree, Loras College (Roman Catholic), Dubuque, Iowa.
12/02/72 Spiritualist Minister, ADL
02/02/73 1st Degree (Alexandrian Tradition) Witch
03/21/73 1st Degree "Member" (Druidic Rite) Witch
06/22/73 2nd Degree "Priesthood of Mechizedek"(Druidic)
07/22/73 3rd Degree "High Priesthood of Melchizedek (Druidic)
07/29/73 Sealed "For Time and Eternity" (Druidic marriage ceremony or "handfasting")
09/22/73 2nd and 3rd Degrees "High Priest and Magus"- (Alexandrian Rite)
05/01/74 "Wizard" (Druidic Rite)
05/31/74 Legally married
12/22/74 4th Degree "Practicus" (Alexandrian)
04/30/75 1st Degree "Member" (Church of Satan)
12/14/75 Ordained to Catholic Diaconate, American National Catholic Church (Old Catholic Rite)
01/15/76 Ordained to Catholic Priesthood, American National Catholic Church
02/02/76 5th Degree "Adeptus Minor" (Alexandrian)
05/20/76 1st Degree Entered Apprentice" (Masonry)
09/20/76 2nd Degree "Fellowcraft" (Masonry)
11/24/76 3rd Degree "Master Mason" (Masonry)
03/26/77 4th-7th Degrees "Royal Arch" (York Rite Masonry)
03/26/77 8th Degree "Super Excellent Master (York Rite Masonry)

04/02/77 9th- 10 Degree "Knight Order of Temple" (York Rite Masonry)

04/30/77 2nd Degree "Warlock" (Church of Satan—same as 6th Degree Alexandrian"Adeptus Major")

07/23/77 7th Degree Gnostic Bishop (Grand Master of the Temple Oto)

09/15/77 90th Degree (Memphis Mizraim)

10/31/78 "Priest" (Church of Satan)

06/01/79 First Degree "Lava Tete" (Voodoo)

10/31/79 Fourth Degree "Pontiff Cardinal" (Church of Satan-Italian Jurisdiction)

12/15/79 2nd Degree "Houngan" (Voodoo)

08/08/80 Mormon Baptism

09/20/80 Shrine "Noble" (Masonry)

10/31/80 5th Degree "Pontiff Hierophant" (Church of Satan— same as 8th Degree Alexandrian)

10/31/80 14th Degree "Lodge of Perfection" (Scottish Rite Masonry)

11/01/80 16th Degree "Prince of Jerusalem" (Scottish Rite Masonry)

11/01/80 18th Degree "Rose Croix of Herdon" (Scottish Rite Masonry)

11/08/80 32nd Degree "Sublime Prince of the Royal Secret" (Scottish Rite Masonry)

12/19/80 Masters of Theology, St. Francis School of Pastoral Ministry (Roman Catholic), Milwaukee

12/22/80 33rd Degree "Grand Sovereign Inspector General" (European or Continental Masonry)

01/01/81 34th Degree "Paladin" (Palladium MasonrY)

05/17/81 Melchizedek Priesthood- "Elder" (Mormon Church)

08/31/81 Sealed and Endowed LDS Temple (Mormon)
10/15/82 Elder's Quorum President (Mormon)
09/14/83 Institute Teacher (Mormon)

06/22/84 SAVED!!!

Saint Francis Seminary

School of Pastoral Ministry

This certifies that

William J. Schnoebelen

having completed all the requirements prescribed by this school is awarded the degree

Master of Theological Studies

In testimony whereof, we have affixed our signatures.

Given at Milwaukee, Wisconsin, this 19th day of December, one thousand nine hundred and eighty.

Rector of Seminary

Dean of Graduate Theology

FRANCIS PETER FACIONE
Dei et Apostolicae Antiochensis Sedis Gratia
Episcopus
Ecclesiae Veteris Romanae Catholicae
pro
Statuibus Mediis Occidentalibus

Universis et singulis praesentes Nostras litteras inspecturis notum facimus atque testamur, Nos hodie Dominica Tertia Adventus Die XIV Mensis Decembris Anni MCMLXXV, Ordinationem Missa Pontificali habentes et Pontificalia exercentes dilectum in Christo Filium

CHRISTOPHER PENDRAGON SYN

per Nos et Nostros examinatores examinatum et adprobatum requisita habentem ad

SACRUM DIACONATUS ORDINEM

juxta Pontificalis praescriptum rite ac recte in Domino promovisse.

In quorum fidem has litteras a Nobis subscriptas sigilloque Nostro munitas expediri jussimus. Datum ex Aedibus Nostris Die XIV Mensis Decembris ,A.D. MCMLXXV.

Episcopus

Assistentibus et Cooperantibus:

Rev. Ralph Adams
Rev. Donald McEvoy
Rev. Theodore Berg
Rev. Edward M. Stehlik

IN THE DISTRICT COURT OF THE STATE OF IOWA, IN AND FOR DUBUQUE COUNTY

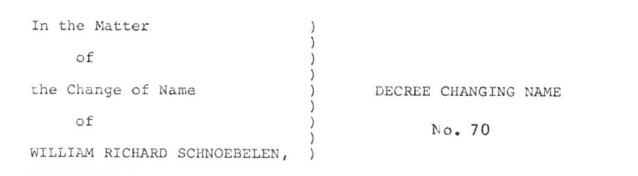

In the Matter)
of)
the Change of Name) DECREE CHANGING NAME
of) No. 70
WILLIAM RICHARD SCHNOEBELEN,)

Now on this 8th day of October, 1973, this matter comes on for determination by the Court on the Petition of WILLIAM RICHARD SCHOEBELEN to have the Court enter a Decree changing his name to CHRISTOPHER PENDRAGON SYN, as provided for in Chapter 674 of the Code of Iowa as amended by Senate File 202 of the Second Regular Session of the 64th General Assembly of the State of Iowa.

NOW, therefore, the Court having been fully advised in the premises and having been fully acquainted with the Petition filed by the said WILLIAM RICHARD SCHNOEBELEN, makes the following finding:

1. That the description of said Petitioner herein is as follows:

    a. Height - 5'11"

    b. Weight - 155 pounds

    c. Color of Hair - Auburn

    d. Color of Eyes - Blue

    e. Race - White

    f. Sex - Male

    g. Date of Birth - August 24, 1949.

    h. Place of Birth - Linn County, Iowa.

2. That the Petitioner has no minor children.

3. That there is no real property which will be affected by this Decree.

WHEREFORE, IT IS HEREBY ORDERED, ADJUDGED, AND DECREED that the said WILLIAM RICHARD SCHNOEBELEN shall be and from now on shall be known as CHRISTOPHER PENDRAGON SYN, and the Clerk of this Court is directed to comply with all the provisios of the law in regard to this change of name.

CERTIFICATE
I, Leroy L. Meyer, Clerk of the District Court of the State of Iowa, in and for Dubuque County, do hereby certify that this is a true and complete copy of the Original instrument filed in this office. IN TESTIMONY WHEREOF, I have hereunto set my hand and affixed the seal of said Court at my office in the 9th day of October, 1973.
Leroy L. Meyer

Karl Kenline
JUDGE, 1st Judicial District of Iowa

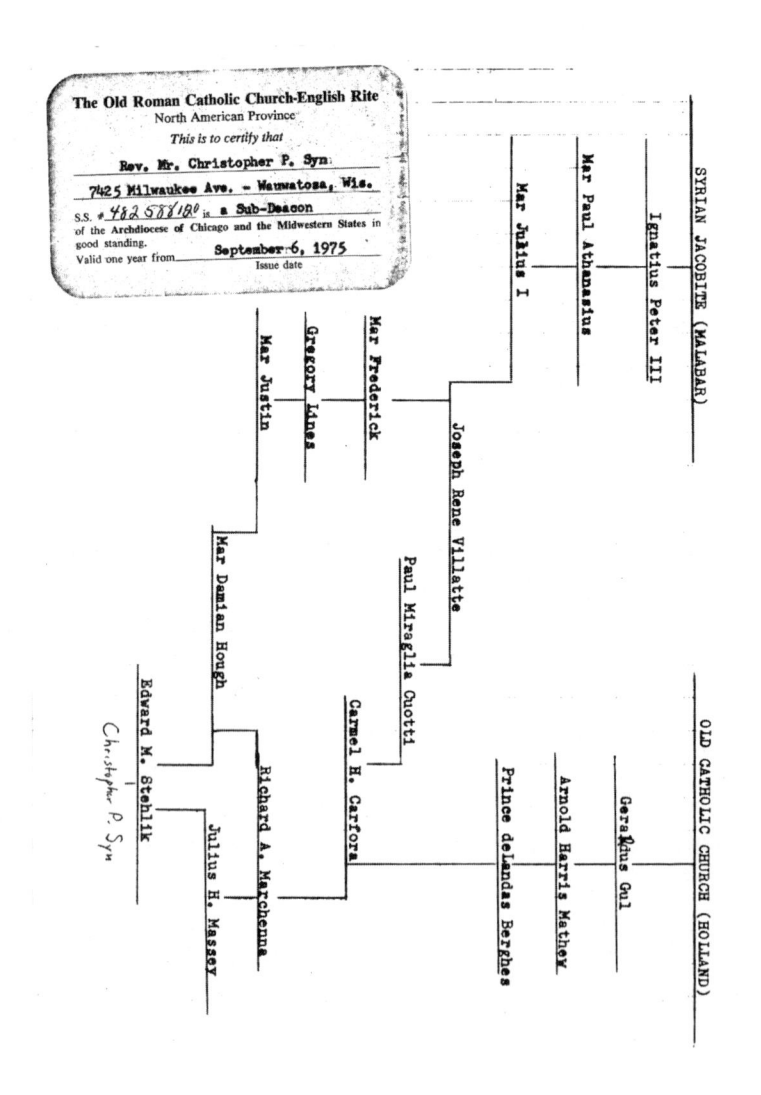

The Old Roman Catholic Church-English Rite
North American Province

This is to certify that

Rev. Mr. Christopher P. Syn

7425 Milwaukee Ave. - Wauwatosa, Wis.

S.S. # 482 58 8180 is **a Sub-Deacon**
of the Archdiocese of Chicago and the Midwestern States in good standing.

Valid one year from **September 6, 1975**
Issue date

SYRIAN JACOBITE (MALABAR)
— Ignatius Peter III
— Mar Paul Athanasius
— Mar Julius I
— Joseph Rene Villatte
— Mar Frederick
— Gregory Lines
— Mar Justin
— Mar Damian Hough
— Edward M. Stehlik
— Christopher P. Syn

— Paul Miraglia Cuotti
— Carmel H. Carfora
— Richard A. Marchenna
— Julius H. Massey

OLD CATHOLIC CHURCH (HOLLAND)
— Gerardus Gul
— Arnold Harris Mathew
— Prince de Landas Berghes

MENTAL SCIENCE INSTITUTE

A Religious Organization
State of Texas Charter No. 244543
P O Box 8832
Minneapolis, Mn. 55408

CERTIFICATE OF ORDINATION

THIS IS TO CERTIFY THAT *Christopher A. P. Syn*
WAS ORDAINED AND APPOINTED A *High Priest*
AFTER THE ORDER OF MELCHIZEDEK BY *D. C. Sh. Taylor*
ON *July 22, 1973* AT *Hattieville, Ark.*
CERTIFIED,

President   *Joan M. Taylor, Secretary*

Grand Lodge
Free and Accepted Masons
of
Wisconsin

To All Free and Accepted Masons Throughout the Globe

FRATERNAL GREETINGS:

In the name of and by authority of the Grand Lodge of Free and Accepted Masons of Wisconsin, we do certify that Brother *CHRISTOPHER P. SYN* was made a Master Mason in *HARTLAND* Lodge No. *122* located at *HARTLAND*, Wisconsin on the *24TH* day of *NOVEMBER*, 19*76*, and passed a satisfactory examination in open lodge in the Work of the Master Mason Degree on the *24TH* day of *MARCH*, 19*77*.

In Testimony Whereof this certificate is issued to him this *24TH* day of *MARCH*, A.D., 1977, A.L. 59*77*.

Richard F. Decker
WORSHIPFUL MASTER

Kenneth G. Sickels
SECRETARY

Attest:

ORDO AB CHAO.

SUPREME COUNCIL

OF S∴ G∴ INSPECTORS GENERAL OF THE A∴A∴ SCOTTISH RITE

FOR THE

Northern Masonic Jurisdiction

OF THE

United States of America, sitting at its General Grand Council, Boston, Massachusetts

This is to certify that Brother **William James Schnobelen** who has signed his name in the margin hereof is a Sublime Prince of the Royal Secret, 32°, and as such is regularly affiliated in our Consistory in the Valley of Milwaukee, in the State of Wisconsin; and is hereby recommended to the protection and fraternal consideration of all members of the Ancient Accepted Scottish Rite throughout the world.

Deus Meumque Jus.

Sov∴ Gr∴ Com∴
Gr∴ Secy∴ Genl∴

Emmanuel... Ch∴
Secretary

73

Certificate of Completion

Witchcraft

LET ALL MEN KNOW THAT

__ Christopher P. Syn __

HAS SATISFIED THE EXAMINERS OF THE School of Wicca

ON THE **20th** DAY OF **Jan.** IN THE GREGORIAN YEAR **1984**

School of Wicca
Blessed Be
Flamen

Be It Known

That having committed to memory and provided sufficient evidence of a working knowledge of Satanic Theology, and undefiled wisdom of the Black Arts, _Christopher P. Syn_, on this _21st_ day of _March_ in the _12th_ year of Our Lord Satan, has been granted the Degree of the _2nd_, that which is called by the name of _Warlock_, and is duly licensed to perform and sustain that which falls within the realm of this Degree as in accord with the tenets and philosophies of

The Church of Satan

having passed before the Council of Nine, Order of the Trapezoid. By all the powers of HELL, So it is DONE.

Anton Szandor LaVey
High Priest & Magus of the Black Order

Elder Certificate of Ordination

This certifies that **WILLIAM JAMES SCHNOEBELEN** of the **Milwaukee Second** Ward/Branch **Milwaukee Wisconsin** Stake/Mission was ordained to the office of Elder in the Melchizedek Priesthood in The Church of Jesus Christ of Latter-day Saints on the **17th** day of **May** Nineteen-hundred and **eighty one**. Ordination performed by **Glen David Ahrens** whose priesthood office is **High Priest**.

Clerk *Franklin Leffler* Stake/Mission/District President

THE CHURCH OF JESUS CHRIST OF LATTER-DAY SAINTS

THE CHURCH OF JESUS CHRIST OF LATTER-DAY SAINTS
Certificate of Baptism and Confirmation

Date **10 AUGUST 19 80**
MILWAUKEE SECOND Ward/Branch **MILWAUKEE WISCONSIN** Stake/Mission

This Certifies that **WILLIAM JAMES SCHNOEBELEN**
SON of **CLETUS JOSEPH SCHNOEBELEN** and **HELEN MAE JAYNE**
Born **24 AUG 1949**, at **CEDAR RAPIDS**, **LINN**, **IOWA**
was baptized **9 AUG 1980**, by **DANNY WESTOVER**, **ELDER**, and confirmed a member of The Church of Jesus Christ of Latter-day Saints, **9 AUG 1980**

by **DANNY WESTOVER**, **ELDER**
Signed *Fred A. Lundberg* Clerk
Signed *[signature]* Bishop/Branch President

TEMPLE SEALING CERTIFICATE

This certifies that WILLIAM JAMES SCHNOEBELEN of Milwaukee, Wisconsin , who were

and ALEXANDRIA Y APPROPE PENDRAGON of Milwaukee, Wisconsin , were sealed by me as husband and wife,

legally married on 31 May 19 74 at Dubuque, Iowa , on the 31st day of August 19 81 .

according to the ordinance of God, for time and for eternity, THE CHURCH OF JESUS CHRIST OF LATTER-DAY SAINTS

In the presence of _Lorenzo Stake Rogero_ Authorized representative of The Church of Jesus Christ of Latter-day Saints
Witness

Patrick D. Jameson SALT LAKE Temple
Witness

The CHURCH OF JESUS CHRIST OF LATTER-DAY SAINTS

Temple Recommend

EXPIRES LAST DAY **NOV '84**

First name: William Initial: J. Last name: Schnoebelen
Ward: Milwaukee 2nd Unit number: 0150746
Stake-Mission: Milwaukee Wisconsin Unit number: 504133

Ordinances involved must be initialed by the issuer

All ordinances for living/dead — Baptisms for dead only — ☒ Male ☐ Female — Birth (day, month): 24 Aug

Signature of applicant

Signature of bishop/branch president

Signature of member of stake presidency or mission president

Date issued (day, month, year): 2 Nov. 1983

Order additional copies of Mormonism's Temple of Doom

Online
BeyondMormonism.com
HolyMurder.com

Request Jim Spencer's Free Newsletter

Phone

Retail Orders
800-871-7120

Bookstores
and
Quantity Discounts
800-788-8354
(FAX 208-322-7205)

Mail
Spencer Books
Box 9017
Boise, ID 82707
jim@BeyondMormonism.com

Other Books

Beyond Mormonism:
An Elder's Story
(BeyondMormonism.com)

Holy Murder:
Polygamy's Blood

Have you Witnessed to a
Mormon Lately?

Hard Case Witnessing:
Winning "Impossibles"
for Christ

Heresy Hunters:
Character Assassination
in the Church

Whited Sepulchers
The Hidden Language
of the Temple